THE CITIZENSHIP DEBATE
CAA & NRC

Amit Malviya, a former banker, is currently the National Head-Information & Technology of the Bharatiya Janata Party.

Salman Khurshid is an Indian politician, designated senior advocate, eminent author and a law teacher.

THE CITIZENSHIP DEBATE
CAA & NRC

A Case of

Misreading   Misdirection

AMIT MALVIYA   SALMAN KHURSHID

RUPA

Published by
Rupa Publications India Pvt. Ltd 2020
7/16, Ansari Road, Daryaganj
New Delhi 110002

Sales centres:
Allahabad Bengaluru Chennai
Hyderabad Jaipur Kathmandu
Kolkata Mumbai

Copyright A Case of Misreading © Amit Malviya 2020
A Case of Misdirection © Salman Khurshid 2020

All rights reserved.

No part of this publication may be reproduced, transmitted, or stored in a retrieval system, in any form or by any means, electronic, mechanical, photocopying, recording or otherwise, without the prior permission of the publisher.

The views and opinions expressed in this book are the authors' own and the facts are as reported by them which have been verified to the extent possible, and the publishers are not in any way liable for the same.

ISBN: 978-93-8996-798-2

First impression 2020

10 9 8 7 6 5 4 3 2 1

The moral right of the authors has been asserted.

Printer at HT Media Ltd, Gr. Noida

This book is sold subject to the condition that it shall not, by way of trade or otherwise, be lent, resold, hired out, or otherwise circulated, without the publisher's prior consent, in any form of binding or cover other than that in which it is published.

Contents

A Case of Misreading by Amit Malviya / 1

A Case of Misdirection by Salman Khurshid /105

Index / 191

A CASE OF MISREADING

Amit Malviya

To the millennia-old civilization that is Bharatvarsh

Author's Note

I would like to thank Professor Ramesh Rao for his feedback and Sudhanva Bedekar for research inputs.

Introduction to CAA and NRC

In December 2019, the Indian Parliament passed the Citizenship (Amendment) Act, 2019 (hereinafter, CAA). As a result, a much-heated debate ensued. Several Opposition parties, vested interest groups, lobbies and stakeholders have agitated and attacked the CAA with vehemence. It is alleged that the CAA and the proposed National Register of Citizens (NRC) are a direct attack on the secular credentials of India. Every attempt has been made to show that the said exercise is in furtherance of the 'Hindutva' agenda of the ruling Bharatiya Janata Party (BJP).

It is argued that since the CAA excludes Muslims from its ambit, it violates Article 14 of the Constitution of India and also that it is contrary to the 'basic structure' of the Constitution. In this context, it is important to note that the United States (US) has a social security system that keeps track of its entire population. So do other countries that have their own unique systems to identify, list and track their citizens. Pakistan's National Database and Registration Authority (NADRA) maintains population records. According to the United Nations (UN) Department of Economic and Social Affairs,

> Population registers have consolidated their status as a reality in several countries, especially those of northern Europe, where they have become an important source

of information for various statistical surveys, including the population Census. Population registers have been effectively used as a statistical data source for decades and they may be considered the logical product of the evolution of a vital statistics system.[1]

As per the UN,

> It has to be stressed that the primary function of the population register is to provide reliable information for the administrative purposes of government, particularly for programme planning, budgeting and taxation. The registers are also useful in other administrative areas, such as establishing personal identification, voting, education and military service, social insurance and welfare, and for police and court reference. Register information is also utilized for issuing documents needed for the admission of children to nurseries, kindergartens and schools and the assignment of residents to health clinics.[2]

We will consider and comment upon all these arguments. However, as a first step, it is necessary to understand what the CAA and NRC are.

What is CAA

The CAA received its assent from the President of India on 12 December 2019, and subsequently came to be published in the

---

[1] Available at: https://unstats.un.org/unsd/demographic/sources/popreg/popregmethods.htm. Last accessed on 23 March 2020.
[2] Available at: https://unstats.un.org/unsd/demographic/sources/popreg/popregmethods.htm. Last accessed on 23 March 2020.

official gazette. It is a three-page legislation with far-reaching consequences. It is necessary to discuss in detail the provisions contained in the CAA. An amendment has been made to Section 2(1)(b) of the Citizenship Act, 1955, which defines an 'illegal migrant'. The amendment to Section 2(1)(b) is in the nature of a proviso. In legal parlance, a proviso is a conditional stipulation that derives from the general rule contained in the provision. Before dealing with the proviso added to Section 2(1)(b) that defines 'illegal migrant', it is pertinent to peruse Section 2(1)(b), which reads as follows:

> 2(1)(b) 'illegal migrant' means a foreigner who has entered into India—
>
> (i) without a valid passport or other travel documents and such other document or authority as may be prescribed by or under any law in that behalf; or
> (ii) with a valid passport or other travel documents and such other document or authority as may be prescribed by or under any law in that behalf but remains therein beyond the permitted period of time

A simple reading of the definition of the term 'illegal migrant' makes it clear that it includes two categories of persons: first, those who enter India without a passport or other travel documents; and second, those who enter validly, with documents, but continue to stay beyond the prescribed period. To this definition, a proviso has been added. The proviso added to the CAA 2019 [Proviso, S. 2(1) (b)] reads as follows:

> Provided that any person belonging to Hindu, Sikh, Buddhist, Jain, Parsi or Christian community from

Afghanistan, Bangladesh or Pakistan, who entered into India on or before the 31st day of December 2014 and who has been exempted by the Central Government by or under clause (c) of sub-section (2) of section 3 of the Passport (Entry into India) Act, 1920 or from the application of the provisions of the Foreigners Act, 1946 or any rule or order made thereunder, shall not be treated as illegal migrant for the purposes of this Act.

It is clear that this proviso carves out an exception for members of major non-Muslim religious groups from Afghanistan, Pakistan and Bangladesh who have entered India on or before 31 December 2014. It is often argued that the CAA neither makes any mention of migrants facing religious persecution nor does it give any rationale for the December 2014 cut-off. It is, however, necessary to read the proviso quoted above along with the provisions of the Passport (Entry into India) Act, 1920 and the Foreigners Act, 1946, which were amended and notified on 7 September 2015,[3] in order to understand its true import. The said amendments gave a one-time amnesty of sorts to those migrants who fled religious persecution in these three neighbouring Islamic republics and sought shelter in India before 31 December 2014, and did not have the necessary documents. To regularize/provide administrative support to instances of religious minorities from these countries, the Union Government has, since December 2014, started issuing long-term visas as per a 2012 policy of the United Progressive

---

[3] Amendment to the Passport and Foreigners Act dated 7 September 2015, available at: https://www.prsindia.org/sites/default/files/bill_files/Foreigners_Act_and_Passport_Act_Notification_September_2015_0.pdf. Last accessed on 10 April 2020.

Alliance (UPA) government. These three countries have been identified as an area of transmigration of populations by the Act, and validly serves as a rationale for the legislation.

The next significant amendment is the insertion of Section 6B. The provision reads as follows:

> 6B. (1) The Central Government or an authority specified by it in this behalf may, subject to such conditions, restrictions and manner as may be prescribed, on an application made in this behalf, grant a certificate of registration or certificate of naturalisation to a person referred to in the proviso to clause (b) of sub-section (1) of section 2. (2) Subject to fulfilment of the conditions specified in section 5 or the qualifications for naturalisation under the provisions of the Third Schedule, a person granted the certificate of registration or certificate of naturalisation under sub-section (1) shall be deemed to be a citizen of India from the date of his entry into India. (3) On and from the date of commencement of the Citizenship (Amendment) Act, 2019, any proceeding pending against a person under this section in respect of illegal migration or citizenship shall stand abated on conferment of citizenship to him: Provided that such person shall not be disqualified for making application for citizenship under this section on the ground that the proceeding is pending against him and the Central Government or authority specified by it in this behalf shall not reject his application on that ground if he is otherwise found qualified for grant of citizenship under this section: Provided further that the person who makes the application for citizenship under this section shall not

be deprived of his rights and privileges to which he was entitled on the date of receipt of his application on the ground of making such application. (4) Nothing in this section shall apply to tribal area of Assam, Meghalaya, Mizoram or Tripura as included in the Sixth Schedule to the Constitution and the area covered under 'The Inner Line' notified under the Bengal Eastern Frontier Regulation, 1873.

Again, a plain reading of the provision makes clear that sub-sections (1), (2) and (3) give effect to the mandate of the proviso contained in Section 2(1)(b) by ensuring that the persons belonging to the religious groups mentioned therein may get the status of a citizen of India. Sub-section (1) provides for grant of certificate of registration or naturalization to the persons contained in the proviso to Section 2(1)(b) which has been referred above. Sub-section (2) declares that such an individual, on fulfilment of certain conditions, shall be deemed to be a citizen of India from the date of his entry into the territory of India. Sub-section (3) effectively puts an end to proceedings pertaining to illegal migration or citizenship pending against such individuals. Sub-section (4) excludes certain areas in Northeast India. Understood simply, Section 6B makes it clear that the Government of India can grant citizenship to those people under the proviso contained in Section 2(1)(b).

Apart from the two provisions added by the CAA, which we have discussed above, there are certain other minor additions that are in furtherance of the provisions discussed earlier.

What are NRC and NPR

There is widespread confusion regarding the link between CAA, National Population Register (NPR) and NRC. This confusion will have to be addressed and clarified. The CAA, as pointed out earlier, carves out an exemption to the definition of the term 'illegal migrant' and extends citizenship rights to those individuals who have been exempted under the proviso contained therein. There is also some confusion regarding the difference between NPR and the Census. It is necessary to note that the two are not one and the same. The Census is an enumeration process which is carried out under the provisions of the Census Act, 1948, every 10 years. The NPR, on the other hand, contains data of the usual residents of a particular place. Residents may or may not be citizens of India.

A notification pertaining to the commencement of the house listing for the purpose of Census was issued by the Central Government on 7 January 2020. It reads as follows:

> In exercise of the powers conferred by Section 3 and Section 17-A of the Census Act, 1948, read with Rule 6A of the Census Rules, 1990, the Central Government hereby declares that the house-listing operations of the Census of India, 2021, shall take place from 1 April 2020 to 30 September 2020 in India.[4]

Subsequent to this notification, another notification issued on the same day enlists the questions which are to be asked by

---

[4] Ministry of Home Affairs (Office of the Registrar General, India) Notification, S.O. 119(E), 7 January 2020.

the Census officers while conducting the Census.[5] The Census is thus a process of collection of statistical data which shall include the various characteristics of persons included in the exercise. Census 2021 will be the 16th National Census since 1872, and eighth since Independence.

The exercise of NPR and NRC, on the other hand, are governed by the Citizenship (Registration of Citizens and Issue of National Identity Cards) Rules, 2003, which were notified on 3 December 2004, when the Congress-led UPA government was in office. The term 'population register' has been defined by these rules. Rule 2(l) defines the term 'population register' as '...the register containing details of persons usually residing in a village or rural area or town or ward or demarcated area (demarcated by the Registrar General of Citizen Registration) within a ward in a town or urban area.' The NRC is a database of the citizens of India. The NRC, or the National Register of Indian Citizens (NRIC), is to be prepared by the Registrar General of Citizen Registration. The legislative mandate in this regard is contained in Section 14A of the Citizenship Act, 1955. Section 14A reads as follows:

> 14A. Issue of national identity cards—(1) The Central Government may compulsorily register every citizen of India and issue national identity card to him. (2) The Central Government may maintain a National Register of Indian Citizens and for that purpose establish a National Registration Authority. (3) On and from the date of commencement of the Citizenship (Amendment) Act,

---

[5] Ministry of Home Affairs (Office of the Registrar General, India) Notification, S.O. 120(E), 7 January 2020.

2003 (6 of 2004), the Registrar General, India, appointed under sub-section (1) of section 3 of the Registration of Births and Deaths Act, 1969 (18 of 1969) shall act as the National Registration Authority and he shall function as the Registrar General of Citizen Registration. (4) The Central Government may appoint such other officers and staff as may be required to assist the Registrar General of Citizen Registration in discharging his functions and responsibilities. (5) The procedure to be followed in compulsory registration of the citizens of India shall be such as may be prescribed.

Rule 2(k) defines the term 'National Register of Indian Citizens' as '...the register containing details of Indian citizens living in India and outside India.'

Rule 3 provides that the Registrar General of Citizens shall establish and maintain the NRC. It also provides that the NRC shall be further divided into a state register, a district register, a subdistrict register and a local register. These registers, it is provided, shall contain such details as the Central Government may, in consultation with the Registrar General of Citizens, prescribe. Rule 3(3) provides that the following details will be contained in such a register:

(i) Name; (ii) Father's name; (iii) Mother's name; (iv) Sex; (v) Date of birth; (vi) Place of birth; (vii) Residential address (present and permanent); (viii) Marital status ñ if ever married, name of the spouse; (ix) Visible identification mark; (x) Date of registration of citizen; (xi) Serial number of registration; and (xii) National identity number.

The confusion about the distinction between NPR and NRC will now be addressed. Rule 3 is titled as 'National Register of Indian Citizens' and, as pointed out earlier, it provides that the Registrar General shall maintain the NRC. The question arises as to where, then, is the mandate for an NPR and what exactly is the distinction? Sub-rule (4) of Rule 3 provides for the preparation of the 'Population Register'. It stipulates that the Central Government may, by an order issued in this regard, decide a date by which the population register shall be prepared by collecting information relating to all persons who are usually residing within the jurisdiction of the Local Registrar. The definition of the term 'population register' has been quoted above. It is distinct from the definition of NRIC. Thus, the provision which is directly concerned with NPR is Rule 3(4). Now, Rule 4 provides that the Central Government shall, for the purpose of NRC, carry out a house-to-house enumeration for collection of the necessary data. There are provisions for the verification of the data by the local registrar. It is provided by sub-rule (4) of Rule 4, that particulars of such individuals whose citizenship is doubtful will be entered by the local registrar with an appropriate remark, and further enquiry may be carried out. It is here, that the reference to 'doubtful' emerges. It is necessary to clarify that this 'marking as doubtful' pertains to the preparation of NRC and not the 'Population Register', a point that is often made by critics of the NPR.

On 4 February 2020, while answering a question raised in the Lok Sabha by Congress' Member of Parliament (MP) Manish Tewari, Minister of State for Home Affairs Nityanand Rai clarified that no verification is done in the process of updating the NPR, to find individuals whose citizenship is doubtful. It was also clarified that no decision was taken to prepare the NRIC at the national level. Subsequently, Home Minister Amit Shah, also on 12 February 2020, clearly stated on the floor of the Rajya Sabha that no person would be marked as doubtful during the NPR process. Sub-rule 5 provides an opportunity to any aggrieved individual to be heard before taking a final decision of including or excluding the person from the Register. Sub-rule 6 provides for the publication of a draft register by the subdistrict or Taluka Registrar and allows for objections. A significant provision of these rules is Rule 5, which has made it very clear that every official of the Central Government, state government, local bodies or their undertakings shall assist the Registrar General of Citizen Registration or any person authorized by her/him in her/his behalf, in preparation of the database relating to each family and every person, and in implementing the provisions of these rules. It is necessary to take due notice of this provision considering the political pronouncements by several state governments that they will not allow the NPR or NRC to become functional in their state. Rule 6 provides that the process of collecting data and completing the register can be initiated by the Registrar General of Citizens by order in this regard. We cannot fail to notice that the calls for disregarding the NPR and NRC exercises have been under the guise of appealing to the 'conscience of the minorities.'

Certain religious groups in the country have been instigated to not take part in the NPR or NRC exercises, and ignore them at the time of implementation. In the wake of this, a reference to Rule 7 becomes imperative:

7. Head of family and individual to act as informant. (1) It shall be compulsory for every Citizen of India to assist the officials responsible for preparation of the National Register of Indian Citizens under rule 4 and get himself registered in the Local Register of Indian Citizens during the period of initialization. (2) It shall be the responsibility of the head of every family, during the period specified for preparation of the Population Register, to give the correct details of name and number of members and other particulars, as specified in sub-rule (3) of rule 3, of the family of which he is the head. (3) It shall be the responsibility of every Citizen to register once with the Local Registrar of Citizen Registration and to provide correct individual particulars to that authority.

It is thus clear that there is a compelling duty cast upon every citizen to provide the required data for the NRC. Rule 8 provides that the registrars tasked with the collection of this information may, by order, require any person to furnish any information within his/her knowledge in connection with the determination of citizenship status of any person, and the person required to furnish information shall be bound to comply with the Registrar's orders. Rule 13 provides for issuance of a national identity card to citizens listed in the NRC.

There are penal consequences for non-compliance with Rules 5, 7, 8, 10, 11 and 14. However, the penalty is in the nature of a fine of up to one thousand rupees. Rule 18 grants the Registrar General of Citizen Registration the power to issue necessary guidelines to state governments.

Considering the provisions listed above, it is necessary to see what progress has been made in this regard. Vide Gazette notification dated 31 July 2019, the Central Government has made it clear that in exercise of powers under Rule 3(4) of the Citizenship Rules, 2003:

> ...the Central Government hereby decides to prepare and update the population register and the field work for house to house enumeration throughout the country except Assam for collection of information relating to all persons who are usually residing within the jurisdiction of local registrar shall be undertaken between the first day of April, 2020 and 30 September, 2020.[6]

The process, on a reading of the notification issued in this regard, is for the preparation and updating of the Population Register and not for the NRC. This notification, it needs to be emphasized yet again, has been brought into force under Rule 3(4), which has been explained earlier. Such a register already exists, and the first such exercise was carried out by the Congress-led UPA government in 2010 and updated in 2015. Congress President Sonia Gandhi and the then President of India, Pratibha Patil, were the first ones to be registered under the NPR. Hence, there is nothing new in the NPR process that should have given rise to a controversy on this scale. Moreover, the Citizenship Rules, 2003, were notified in December 2004, during the Congress party-led UPA regime and hence the party's opposition to what it was once championing is, to put it mildly, baffling. The reasons for the controversy and the apprehensions that certain groups have about the NRC and NPR will be discussed later.

---

[6] Ministry of Home Affairs (Office of the Registrar General Citizen Registration, India) Notification, S.O. 2753(E), 31 July 2019.

As regards completion of the process of NRC, a notification in this regard has been issued only in the context of the state of Assam. Vide a notification dated 31 July 2019,[7] the Central Government (Ministry of Home Affairs, Office of Registrar General of Citizen Registration) had, pursuant to the provisions of Rule 4A(3) of the Citizenship Rules, 2003, enumerated the period for completion of NRC in Assam and had fixed the date of completion of the process by 31 August 2019. This notification mentioned all the earlier notifications issued in this regard and also the time granted for completion. It is thus clear that, as of now, there is no notification for a pan-India NRC. A narrative is being created that pursuant to NRC, detention centres will be set up in the country on a large scale and minorities will be locked up in those detention centres. It is necessary to first make clear that detention centres have existed in the country for decades, much before Prime Minister Narendra Modi came into office. Detention centres are not the same as prisons. If any individual comes to India without requisite documents, or comes with requisite documents but overstays, then he or she would be put in detention centres to be deported later.[8]

There is also some apprehension regarding the information sought under the NPR process. The list of information sought under NPR may increase or decrease from time to time. It is a dynamic exercise necessary to understand the changing demographic profile of the society. In 2010, the following

---

[7] Ministry of Home Affairs (Office of the Registrar General Citizen Registration, India) Notification, S.O. 2752(E), 31 July 2019.

[8] Minister Himanta Biswa Sarma on detention camps in Assam: https://timesofindia.indiatimes.com/india/assam-detention-centres-set-up-on-hc-order-says-himanta-biswa-sarma/articleshow/72946976.cms. Last accessed on 10 April 2020.

information was sought from every resident of the country:

(i) Name of person, (ii) Relationship to head of household, (iii) Father's name, (iv) Mother's name, (v) Spouse's name (if married), (vi) Sex, (vii) Date of birth, (viii) Marital status, (ix) Place of birth, (x) Nationality as declared, (xi) Present address of usual residence, (xii) Duration of stay at present address, (xiii) Permanent residential address, (xiv) Occupation/Activity, and (xv) Educational qualification. Also, three biometrics—photograph, 10 fingerprints and two iris images—were collected in selected states allocated to the Office of Registrar General for persons of age five years and above, for the purpose of de-duplication and generation of Aadhaar number through UIDAI.

Aadhaar number, mobile phone number, Permanent Account Number (PAN), Voter ID card number, driver's licence number and passport number (Indian passport only) were the additional fields included in pre-test of NPR 2020, besides place of last residence, and date and place of birth of father and mother of the resident.

These are data points required in order to keep track of the changing socio-economic conditions. By linking NPR with registration of birth and death, a real-time population register would be available, leading to a register-based Census in the future. NPR data can be used for transparent and efficient delivery of social benefits by linking with various beneficiary-oriented government schemes. For instance, the Socio-Economic Caste Census (SECC) is based on the NPR data, which was subsequently used for deciding different types of beneficiaries, strengthening the overall framework of the system. Household-wise NPR data was used for better targeting of schemes such as Ayushman Bharat Yojana, Pradhan Mantri

Jan Dhan Yojana, Pradhan Mantri Awas Yojana, Pradhan Mantri Ujjwala Yojana, Saubhagya scheme, etc. NPR 2010 data was shared for ensuring the efficacy of the Public Distribution System (PDS) in a few states.

Imagine, if a number of Telugu-speaking people migrate to Gujarat, the state administration would need reliable data set to understand this trend of social migration, the reason(s) for such migration and the socio-economic background of the people before it can tailor social welfare programmes and policies for such a migrant population, who have decided to make Gujarat their home state. For instance, does it need to provide option for education in Telugu? Will they need state support to build their lives in a new place? What about accommodation, sanitation, health and education? Unless the governments, both central and state, have such data, how will they be in a position to shape their economic and social policies (for migrants) effectively? Therefore, those opposing the NPR exercise are essentially doing a disservice to the poor and the new middle class.

What is the Link between CAA and NRC

From a legalistic point of view, it is clear that there is no link between the CAA and the NRC exercise. A perusal of the relevant provisions of the CAA make it abundantly clear that the CAA is a law that grants citizenship rights to the persecuted minorities of Pakistan, Bangladesh and Afghanistan who migrated to India before 31 December 2014. The CAA is certainly not a law that takes away citizenship of any individual. It also does not confer a direct right of citizenship, even to the persecuted communities mentioned in the law. It merely gives them amnesty from the crime of illegally migrating to India.

The CAA has no bearing on individuals already residing in India and who are citizens of India, whatever their religious affiliation. The NRC, on the other hand, is an exercise to create a register of Indian citizens. The argument that the CAA and the NRC are interlinked is based on certain fears and apprehensions that are politically motivated and instigated by those seeking to undermine the present government.

The critics argue that after the NRC exercise is notified, a wholly hypothetical argument since there is no notification just yet, some citizens in India won't be able to furnish all the required documents (since many Indians apparently do not maintain all their documents or do not have all the requisite documents), and they shall then become illegal migrants and get sent to detention centres. They surmise, wrongly, that grave injustice would be done to Muslims, because non-Muslims, who cannot submit documents will have the CAA come to their rescue as the legislation purports to grant immunity to members of the non-Muslim religious group. They would then have to simply prove, in accordance to the new law, that they have been residing in India for a period of five years. This is, however, an unsound argument. For it to have any credibility, it would have to be demonstrated that among the existing set of people residing in India, more Muslims than non-Muslims will have difficulty proving their citizenship. But those who have consistently thrived on insecurities of the Muslims have gone a step further and called it an exercise to weed out and deport (from India) Muslims who do not have the required documents. Nothing can be farther from the truth though.

Let us look at this debate from another angle. Assume there is an NRC notification that mandates producing several documents and getting around the process itself requires some effort. In such a situation, should Muslims and non-Muslims alike have difficulty in furnishing the required documents, would the CAA save the latter? The answer is an emphatic no! Let us understand why.

As explained in the beginning of this chapter, the CAA has added a proviso to the definition of an illegal migrant. Some part of it, which is relevant here, is quoted below:

> Provided that any person belonging to Hindu, Sikh, Buddhist, Jain, Parsi or Christian community from Afghanistan, Bangladesh or Pakistan, who entered into India on or before the 31st day of December, 2014...

It is thus apparent that Hindu, Sikh, Buddhist, Jain or Christian communities 'from Afghanistan, Bangladesh or Pakistan' are to be protected.

Thus, if Indian Muslims and non-Muslims alike are not able to produce certain documents, which may potentially jeopardize their citizenship rights, then it is not true that CAA would save the day for the non-Muslims. To be eligible for any protection under the CAA, non-Muslims, or members of those religious groups that find specific mention in the CAA, would have to follow all the rules and procedures prescribed in the CAA and prove that they migrated from Afghanistan, Bangladesh or Pakistan. If, in a rare case, someone with dubious antecedents does manage to get past the authorities and all the processes, and acquires a citizenship through the CAA route, Section 10 of the Citizenship Amendment

Act, 1955, authorizes the government to revoke it on grounds of false representation.[9] Thus, this argument too is misconceived.

If at all there is any procedure that casts a higher burden for proving citizenship on members of one religious group over another, then such a procedure would undoubtedly be struck down on the anvil of Article 14 of the Constitution of India, which guarantees equality before law and equal protection under the laws.

Some have also held the view that the NPR exercise, which has already been notified, is a stepping stone to the NRC. It is argued that as per the rules, these citizens (who are not able to produce all the documents) will be 'marked out' in the NPR for further enquiry. The NPR data will then be included in the Local Register as is contemplated by the Citizenship Rules, 2003, and those not included in the said data may then not feature in the NRC.[10] This controversy, of individuals being marked as non-citizens or having doubtful identity during the NPR exercise, as explained earlier in this, is without any basis. Home Minister Amit Shah, speaking in the Parliament on 12 February 2020, referred to the appropriate provision in law, which is unequivocal on the matter, and debunked the misplaced arguments.

---

[9] Section 10 of the Citizenship Amendment Act, 1955, available at: https://www.tiss.edu/uploads/files/Citizenship_Act_1955.pdf. Last accessed on 10 April 2020.

[10] Prasanna Mohanty, 'CAA & NRC II: Here are the myths and facts about all-India National Register of Citizens', *Business Today*, 24 December 2019, available at: https://www.businesstoday.in/current/economy-politics/caa-nrc-national-register-of-citizens-myths-and-facts-citizenship-amendment-act-modi-amit-shah-govt/story/392474.html. Last accessed on 6 March 2020.

Regarding NRC, it is evident that the Citizenship Rules, 2003, only require 'correct particulars' to be mentioned. Neither the Citizenship Rules, 2003, nor any other notification or guidelines in this regard makes any mention of the need to submit any document during the entire process. The only responsibility cast upon the respondents of these surveys is that they give the correct particulars of their residency.

This gets us to the often-heard phrase, *'Hum kagaz nahin dikhayenge.'* It almost became like a war cry of the misplaced dissent against the humanitarian CAA. Those who took to the streets either had no idea or were misled by their handlers into believing that they would have to produce some 'kagaz', and failing to do so would lead to their citizenship being stripped and worse. Now that it is clear that there is no notification or rule that mandates producing any specific set of document(s) in the first place, one realizes how vile, malicious and politically expedient the anti-CAA campaign has been. But if one just assumed that a future notification pertaining to the NRC, as is being speculated, does stipulate onerous conditions, then could it be argued that it will only put the Muslims at a disadvantage? In any case, isn't it too far-fetched to believe that there would be individuals who would not even have a single document? At this point, however, since the first argument itself is fallacious and premature, it may be futile to even spend a thought over the second assertion.

Further, it is facetious to even suggest that once a person's citizenship is marked doubtful, he/she automatically ends up losing his/her citizenship without an appeal or legal remedy at his/her disposal. The rules contemplate the hearing of objections and provide enough safeguards against arbitrary exercise of power. The argument of arbitrariness propagated by the Opposition rests on the premise that the registrars and officials entrusted with the task of carrying out this exercise are either inefficient or are politically motivated. Such distrust of authorities and officials, without cogent and valid reasons, is motivated and espoused by certain political/interest groups, who are working with the sole objective of derailing the entire process.

The CAA challenge is now in the Apex Court. One can be reasonably sure that an enabling notification, likely at a future date, pertaining to the NRC too will be a subject of raging political controversy and judicial challenge. The matter of ascertaining constitutional validity of the entire exercise eventually may have to be decided by the courts. In the meanwhile, a detailed discussion regarding the constitutional validity of the CAA as also the Citizenship Rules, 2003, shall follow in the ensuing chapters.

Documents Define Your Identity

After the passage of the CAA, many have speculated that the NRC exercise is also in the pipeline and would soon become a reality. In the previous chapter, we pointed out that the NPR notification has already been published in the official gazette. There has also been a perusal of the Citizenship Rules, 2003, which contain the relevant provisions pertaining to the NRC and NPR. It is also clear that NPR is a preliminary exercise before carrying out the entire NRC exercise. Though the Government of India has said that currently, there are no plans for a nationwide NRC,[11] it is clear that since the NPR is a preliminary and necessary step in this direction, the government may also push for a nationwide NRC in due course.

At the moment, the NRC exercise is being carried out only in the state of Assam under the supervision of the Supreme Court of India.[12] There is a background to this. In Assam, there were widespread agitations against the big influx of illegal migrants from Bangladesh, which led to the signing of the

---

[11] 'No talks on nationwide NRC right now, PM Modi was right, says Amit Shah', *India Today*, 24 December 2019, available at: https://www.indiatoday.in/india/story/no-talks-on-nationwide-nrc-now-amit-shah-interview-1631224-2019-12-24. Last accessed on 10 March 2020.

[12] Assam Sanmilita Mahasangha vs Union of India and Others, (2015) 3 SCC 1.

Assam Accord between the All Assam Students' Union (AASU) and the Central Government in 1985. The issue of illegal migration and demographic invasion in Assam has a historical context, and Pakistan's failure to get Assam included in East Pakistan in 1947 has remained a source of resentment among the Pakistani establishment. Zulfikar Ali Bhutto, the ninth prime minister of Pakistan, who was hanged to death in his own country, in his book, *The Myths of Independence*, wrote, 'It would be wrong to think that Kashmir is the only dispute that divides India and Pakistan, though undoubtedly the most significant. One at least is nearly as important as the Kashmir dispute, that of Assam and some districts of India adjacent to East Pakistan. To these, Pakistan has very good claims.'[13]

Immediately after India's Partition, realizing that migration from erstwhile East Pakistan (now Bangladesh) into Assam was a grim reality, and some of them (non-Muslim migrants) needed protection and should not be expelled from Assam, Prime Minister Jawaharlal Nehru's government enacted the Immigrants (Expulsion from Assam) Act, 1950. Section 2 of this Act[14] provides for expulsion of immigrants from Assam to then Pakistan, but a proviso in the section excludes expulsion of immigrants, essentially non-Muslims, without being specific:

> Provided that nothing in this section shall apply to any person who on account of civil disturbances or the fear of such disturbances in any area now forming part of

---

[13] Zulfikar Ali Bhutto, *The Myth of Independence*, p. 138, reproduced by Sani Panhwar, available at: http://www.sanipanhwar.com/The%20 Myth%20of%20Independence%20by%20Zulfikar%20Ali%20Bhutto.pdf.
[14] Available at: https://indiacode.nic.in/bitstream/123456789/1674/1/A1950-10.pdf. Last accessed on 14 April 2020.

Pakistan has been displaced from or has left his place of residence in such area and who have been subsequently residing in Assam.

That this section was meant to protect Hindu migrants is clearly evident not only from the language of the proviso but also from the contemporaneous parliamentary debates surrounding this legislation.

Assam was not the only state bearing the burden of massive migration of minorities from East Pakistan; there was West Bengal too. BJP founder, Dr S.P. Mookerjee, in a statement in the Parliament on 19 April 1950, on his resignation as minister of industries and supplies from Prime Minister Nehru's Cabinet, said:

> For instance, I along with others, gave assurances to the Hindus of East Bengal, stating that if they suffered at the hands of the future Pakistan government, if they were denied elementary rights of citizenship, if their lives and honour were jeopardised or attacked, Free India would not remain an idle spectator and their just cause would be boldly taken up by the government and people of India.
>
> Let us not forget that the Hindus of East Bengal are entitled to the protection of India, not on humanitarian considerations alone, but by virtue of their sufferings and sacrifices, made cheerfully for generations, not for advancing their own parochial interests, but for laying the foundations of India's political freedom and intellectual progress.
>
> Islamic State is Pakistan's creed and a planned extermination of Hindus and Sikhs and expropriation of their properties constitute its settled policy. As a result of

this policy, life for the minorities in Pakistan has become nasty, brutish and short. Let us not be forgetful of the lessons of history. We will do so at our own peril. I am not talking of bygone times, but if anyone analyses the course of events in Pakistan since creation, it will be manifest that there is no honourable place for Hindus within that State. The problem is not communal. It is essentially political.[15]

There was a clear recognition even back in 1950 that the non-Muslim minorities in Pakistan were not safe and had to be protected, and that constituted our civilizational and humanitarian responsibility. Given the historical religious basis for the Partition, and the insistence of the Muslim League and its constituents, who, in the provincial elections of 1946, voted overwhelmingly (with 89.5 per cent votes, the Muslim League was elected to 429 of the 492 seats reserved for Muslims, and a meagre 4.4 per cent of Indian Muslims voted for the Congress party) in favour of Mohammad Ali Jinnah's call for creation of a separate Islamic State of Pakistan on religious lines, there was acknowledgement of this religious divide between Hindus and Muslims, even when Abul Kalam Azad, a Muslim, was the president of the Congress party.

The experience, in short, has been that religious minorities in the neighbouring Islamic Republic of Pakistan and Bangladesh require protection, when they flee religious persecution and come to India. The Citizenship Amendment Act takes forward the early initiative of the Congress government in 1950, which

---

[15] Parliamentary Debates, Part 2-proceedings other than questions & answers, Wednesday, 19 April 1950. Statement by Dr S.P. Mookerjee on his resignation as minister of industries and supplies, pp 3017–22.

was then only confined to Assam.

The Assam Accord, which comes much later in time and against the backdrop of illegal migration that was mostly migration of Muslims, declared that foreigners who had come to Assam on or after 25 March 1971, would be detected, deleted from electoral rolls and expelled according to the law.[16] The Parliament, under former Prime Minister Indira Gandhi's leadership, had also passed the Illegal Migrants (Determination by Tribunal) Act, 1983 (hereinafter referred to as the IMDT Act), which was applicable only to the state of Assam and contained a provision to expel Bangladeshis from the state of Assam. However, the procedure contained in the Assam Accord was such that it would make it practically impossible for the authorities to expel the foreigners. It was hence challenged before the Supreme Court of India and struck down. On 10 April 1992, the then chief minister of Assam, Hiteswar Saikia, gave a statement in the Legislative Assembly that there were 33 lakh (3.3 million) infiltrators from Bangladesh in Assam, which he retracted a few days later. On 14 July 2004, Sriprakash Jaiswal, the then union minister of state for home affairs, made a statement in the Parliament that as on 31 December 2001, there were 50 lakh (5 million) Bangladeshi infiltrators in Assam. This fact is also extracted in the judgement of the Supreme Court rendered in Assam Sanmilita Mahasangha & Ors vs Union of India case dated 17 December 2014:

> On 14 July 2004, in response to an unstarred question pertaining to the deportation of illegal Bangladeshi migrants, the Minister of State, Home Affairs, submitted

---

[16] Clause 5, Assam Accord, 1985.

a statement to Parliament indicating therein that the estimated number of illegal Bangladeshi immigrants into India as on 31 December 2001 was 1.20 crores, out of which 50 lakh were in Assam.

On 16 November 2017, Kiren Rijiju, the then union minister of state for home, made a statement in the Parliament that there were two crore (20 million) Bangladeshi infiltrators in India. No break-up of the numbers for Assam was given.

These figures on illegal migrants in both India and Assam are alarming. However, Assam, unlike the rest of India, has borne the burden of migration for 23 additional years as the Assam Accord, signed by the Rajiv Gandhi government in 1985, sets the cut-off date as 25 March 1971, which is pending determination before the Constitution Bench of the Supreme Court, and has been incorporated in Section 6A of the Citizenship Act as compared to 19 July 1948, for the rest of India. According to three independent studies based on the 2001 and 2011 Census, if illegal migration continues unabated in Assam, the *Khilonjia* (the indigenous people of Assam) will become a minority by 2040, 2047 or 2051. Of the 525 ethnic communities in India, 247 are in the Northeast, with 115 in Assam alone. Migration has rendered a large number of ethnic communities landless, displaced them and is threatening to destroy their identity. Hima Das, the only female athlete from India, who recently won the gold medal for the country in the Women's 400 metres race at the IAAF World under-20 Athletics Championship held at Tampere, Finland, comes from Dhing in Nagaon district, which has over 90 per cent illegal Muslim migrants, who were non-existent in that area over a hundred years ago.

Views of the Apex Court: No Compromise on National Security

The Supreme Court, in the case of Sarbananda Sonowal vs Union of India,[17] struck down the IMDT Act. It held that the Act violated Article 355 of the Constitution of India. Article 355 reads as follows:

> 355. Duty of the Union to protect States against external aggression and internal disturbance. It shall be the duty of the Union to protect every State against external aggression and internal disturbance and to ensure that the government of every State is carried on in accordance with the provisions of this Constitution.

The court thus held that it was the duty of the Central Government to protect the states from external aggression and that illegal Bangladeshis were external aggressors. The court also noted that there was a great demographic shift whereby the population of Muslims in Assam grew by more than 77 per cent between 1971 and 1991. It took note of a report dated 11 August 1998, sent by the governor of Assam to the president of India. Certain observations of the Apex Court in this case are noteworthy. First, the judgement quotes extensively from the governor's report. The report mentions that, 'the illegal migrants coming into India after 1971 have been almost exclusively Muslims.' The report further highlights the following:

> Pakistan's ISI has been active in Bangladesh supporting militant movement in Assam. Muslim militant

---

[17] (2005) 5 SCC 655.

organizations have mushroomed in Assam and there are reports of some 50 Assamese Muslim youths having gone for training to Afghanistan and Kashmir... As a result of population movement from Bangladesh, the spectre looms large of the indigenous people of Assam being reduced to a minority in their home State... The influx of these illegal migrants is turning these districts into a Muslim majority region. It will then only be a matter of time when a demand for their merger with Bangladesh may be made. The rapid growth of international Islamic fundamentalism may provide for driving force for this demand. In this context, it is pertinent that Bangladesh has long discarded secularism and has chosen to become an Islamic State. Loss of lower Assam will severe the entire land mass of the North East, from the rest of India and the rich natural resources of that region will be lost to the Nation.

After an extensive perusal of this report, the Court noted that, 'This being the situation there can be no manner of doubt that the State of Assam is facing "external aggression and internal disturbance" on account of large-scale illegal migration of Bangladeshi nationals.'

It is in this backdrop that the NRC exercise was recently carried out in Assam.

Why the Opposition to Nationwide NRC

There is a great degree of misinformation as well as disinformation in the ranks of the Opposition regarding the NRC, most of it perhaps intentional. In the previous chapter, all the legalities concerning the NRC have already been discussed. The chapter also alludes to the reasons, perhaps briefly, as to why the NRC is being opposed. It is therefore, necessary to ascertain the reasons for opposition to the NRC in some details.

There are several accounts and reports[18] that point to the existence of a large number of illegal Bangladeshis who have illegally infiltrated into India and are staying in large groups in the metropolitan cities of Delhi and Mumbai. It is necessary to deal with these illegal migrants in a strict and organized manner so as to deter continued infiltration in the future. It is for this reason that it is necessary to identify these illegal migrants. The identification process would be streamlined if a nationwide NRIC is created. The problem of illegal Bangladeshis is rampant in the state of West Bengal, among other states. It is alleged that the government of West Bengal is not too keen on taking any action against these illegal migrants since they now serve as a powerful 'vote bank' for the Trinamool Congress (TMC), the party in power in the state, by Chief Minister Mamata Banerjee. Ironically, when she was in the Opposition, she had led the demand for expulsion of illegal Bangladeshi infiltrators from Bengal.[19]

If the NRC is completed, all these illegal migrants, whose presence in the country has been systematically regularized

---

[18] Available at: https://carnegieindia.org/2016/06/29/illegal-immigration-from-bangladesh-to-india-toward-comprehensive-solution-pub-63931. Last accessed on 10 April 2020.

[19] Parliamentary Debate, 2005, Page 183. Mamata Banerjee seeking debate on illegal Bangladeshi migrants in Bengal, available at: https://eparlib.nic.in/bitstream/123456789/785599/1/lsd_14_05_04-08-2005.pdf?fbclid=IwAR3uosaO-mahXLRkpJLpVjJBXz-1hISUiSQbjzmMwKeUUv92yRnEIkhA2xU#search=null%202005. Last accessed on 10 April 2020.

over the years in the name of secularism, by giving them several identity proofs such as Aadhaar and ration card, voter ID, etc., will be sent back to the country of their origin. Furthermore, the demographic imbalances created by these illegal migrants will be resolved. Hence, the opposition to the NRC is motivated and driven by the self-serving agenda of some political actors and assorted activists. The Opposition parties want to portray the NRC exercise as an attempt by the ruling BJP to make India a Hindu nation by stripping Muslims of their citizenship. They have also claimed that the CAA would save non-Muslims from having to prove their citizenship.

These arguments have been adequately addressed in the previous chapter. Some political parties have opposed the NRC, on the ground that it will cause serious inconvenience to the people. That argument is specious because all the citizens will have to go through the process, and not just a select few, and more importantly this exercise is necessary for modernizing and regularizing the population database that is necessary to run an efficient government and ensure internal security. Political rivals of the BJP want to close their eyes to the realities of the day, which includes dealing objectively with the problem of illegal migrants. As to the CAA, it doesn't make any sense to argue that Muslims too should be included in its ambit because it is inconceivable that they would be discriminated against in these Islamic Republic for professing Islam. The CAA is very clear in its remit and intent to protect the minorities in these Muslim-majority neighbourhood countries, where they have faced systematic discrimination and marginalization for decades for simply who they are. It also does not make sense that Bangladeshi Muslims who have come illegally into

India should be protected because they are here for economic reasons and not because of religious persecution. Citizenship rights cannot be extended to them on humanitarian grounds, as some bleeding hearts argue. Doing so would simply open the doors for further illegal migration, and all the attendant social, economic, political and demographic upheavals. Extending citizenship on humanitarian grounds to those who have allegedly migrated due to economic reasons is akin to incentivizing illegal migration, which no sovereign country can afford. Who we let in across our borders is at the sole discretion of the Central Government, which alone has the right to decide on such matters. The law in this regard is clear. This aspect has been addressed in one of the subsequent chapters.

The Supreme Court, in the Sarbananda Sonowal vs Union of India,[20] has already acknowledged this problem as an attack on India's demographic makeup. It has also termed these illegal migrations as a form of external aggression and noted with approval the findings of the report that indicates that these migrants can be a potential security threat. We also cannot ignore the role of Pakistan's Inter-Services Intelligence (ISI) agency in enabling, encouraging and using these illegal migrants for the purpose of fomenting trouble. In light of all this, there can be no doubt that the illegal migrants need to be identified and for which purpose, a nationwide NRC is not only desirable but also necessary.

Some argue that the entire NRC exercise is like searching for a needle in a haystack. Some have also questioned whether illegal immigrants are a threat to India. They have argued that there are several Nepalis illegally staying in India and nobody

---

[20] (2005) 5 SCC 655.

questions them. It is also argued that the NRC has a proven track record of failure.[21] All these criticisms can be easily countered. Regarding Nepalis, it is no one's case that the NRC should selectively target only Bangladeshi or Pakistani Muslims. Moreover, on a practical front, no one would be able to argue that an illegal Bangladeshi or Pakistani migrant is different from an illegal Nepali migrant. All those found overstaying their visas or who are found to have illegally migrated into India need to be deported. As pointed out earlier, the NRC is not selective in its application and hence, this argument is false and frivolous.

The allegation that the track record of NRC is poor is a red herring and needs to be dismissed with the contempt that it deserves. If at all a government agency is not working efficiently, then it is incumbent upon both the political leadership and executive to shape up and demand efficiency. To, therefore, argue that the NRC exercise ought not to be carried out is mischievous. As regards threat to security, posed by illegal migrants, it is no one's claim that religious identity alone is the criterion for identifying those threats.

NRC and National Identity Card

In India, though there are several documents that are used as identity proofs (although they often serve distinct purposes), there is no document that is in the nature of a citizenship identity card. There is no updated population register or

---

[21] Shivam Vij, 'Why India doesn't need NRC', *The Wire*, 22 November 2019, available at: https://theprint.in/opinion/why-india-doesnt-need-nrc/324771/. Last accessed on 11 March 2020.

register of citizens. Citizenship Rules, 2003, which have been discussed in the previous chapter, provide for the issuance of national identity cards. Rule 13 reads as follows:

> 13. Issue of National Identity Cards—The Registrar General of Citizen Registration, or any officer authorized by him in this behalf, shall issue the National Identity Card to every Citizen whose particulars are entered in the National Register of Indian Citizens under sub-rule (3) of rule 3.

These cards will be issued to citizens only when their information is entered into the NRC. Furthermore, Section 14A of the Citizenship Act, 1955, provides that the Central Government may compulsorily register every citizen and issue a national identity card to him/her. The Citizenship Rules, 2003, also make it clear that these cards will be the property of the Central Government. It is important to note that without the assistance of the state governments, it is difficult to implement all this. The Citizenship Rules, 2003, vide Rule 16, provide that the state government shall appoint a Local Registrar of Citizens for each lowest geographical jurisdiction. Furthermore, non-cooperation by the citizens can also create problems, as very limited sanctions are imposed in case of non-compliance. The sanctions are in the nature of a fine of up to one thousand rupees, which is a pittance in these times and can be easily misused/abused. An amendment to this is desirable, because the political scenario in the country would ensure that many citizens and even some state governments may appear reluctant to co-operate with the Central Government in this matter, even though they don't have the constitutional space to do so, defeating the whole purpose of the exercise. A new, robust regime is necessary to meet the needs of the present. However, if the state governments refuse to cooperate, then the Central Government can use the option of invoking Article 356 and imposing President's Rule.

The Assam NRC Exercise

Since the NRC exercise has been carried out in Assam, under the guidance and supervision of the Apex Court, it is necessary to have a look at how the exercise was carried out. The NRC update was a mammoth exercise involving over 52,000 state government officials working for a prolonged period. Hundreds of NRC Seva Kendras (NSKs) were set up to process the documents under the Apex Court's watch. An applicant had to pick any one of the documents under two heads—List A and List B.[22] List A contained the following documents:

1. 1951 NRC
2. Electoral roll(s) up to 24 March (midnight) 1971
3. Land and tenancy records
4. Citizenship certificate
5. Permanent residential certificate
6. Refugee registration certificate
7. Any government issued license/certificate
8. Government service/employment certificate

---

[22] 'Understanding NRC: What it is and if it can be implemented across the country', *The Economic Times*, 23 December 2019, available at: https://economictimes.indiatimes.com/news/et-explains/is-a-pan-india-nrc-possible-the-lesson-from-assam/articleshow/72454225.cms?utm_source=contentofinterest&utm_medium=text&utm_campaign=cppst. Last accessed on 11 March 2020.

9. Bank or post office accounts
10. Birth certificate
11. State educational board or university educational certificate
12. Court records/processes
13. Passport
14. Any LIC policy

List B contained the following documents:

1. Birth certificate
2. Land document
3. Board/university certificate
4. Bank/LIC/post office records
5. Circle officer/gaon panchayat secretary certificate in case of married women
6. Electoral roll
7. Ration card
8. Any other legally acceptable document

It is necessary also to point out as to what were the consequences if a person's name was not included in the NRC. Does it render him remediless? The answer to this question is in the negative. The persons whose names were left out of the NRC had the option of approaching the Foreigners Tribunals. If aggrieved by the order of the Tribunals, then there was an option to file an appeal. The Foreigners Tribunals are constituted under the Foreigners Act, 1946. When a nationwide NRC is compiled, the Foreigners Tribunals will deal with the complaints and challenges. In any case, a nationwide NRC process will not be as complicated as it was in Assam because Assam's was a unique situation.

As regards the Foreigners Tribunals, they are governed by the Foreigners Order, 1964. On 11 June 2019, the Press Information Bureau (PIB), explained all this:

> The Foreigners (Tribunals) Order, 1964 was issued by the Central Government under Section 3 of The Foreigners Act, 1946. It is applicable to the whole country. Major amendments in the Foreigners (Tribunals) Order, 1964 were undertaken in 2013. The last amendment was issued in May, 2019. All these orders are applicable to the whole country and are not specific to any state. Therefore, there is nothing new in this regard in the latest amendment of May 2019. The May 2019 amendment only lays down the modalities for the Tribunals to decide on appeals made by persons not satisfied with the outcome of claims and objections filed against the NRC. Since NRC work is going on only in Assam, therefore, the aforementioned Order, issued on 30th May, 2019 is applicable only to Assam as on date for all practical purposes.[23]

A brief explanation of the Assam NRC and why its efficacy is being questioned is necessary. The ongoing NRC updation process in Assam is regulated by the Citizenship (Registration of Citizens and Issue of National Identity Cards) Rules, 2003, as amended in 2009, and aims to give effect to the Assam Accord of 1985. This is a statutory, transparent and legal process being directly monitored by the Supreme Court of India. The Apex Court has itself set the deadlines for all steps

---

[23] Press Information Bureau, Government of India, Ministry of Home Affairs, available at: https://pib.gov.in/newsite/PrintRelease.aspx?relid=190360. Last accessed on 11 March 2020.

that have been taken so far. The government of Assam as well as the Central Government are acting in accordance with the directives issued by the Supreme Court. The actual NRC updating process started in 2013. Altogether, 3.29 crore people of the state applied for inclusion of their names in the updated NRC. After the due process of claims and objections, a total of 19.06 lakh people were found ineligible for inclusion in the final updated NRC.

The purpose of the exercise was to identify illegal migrants and exclude them from the NRC in the context of Assam, given the provisions of the Assam Accord, but the exercise was challenged and snowballed into a national debate after several questions were raised on the glaring discrepancies, exceptions and omissions.

Upamanyu Hazarika, a senior Supreme Court lawyer, who, the Supreme Court had appointed as a one-man commission to study illegal migration from Bangladesh, in a detailed submission dated 16 August 2018 to the Registrar General & Census Commissioner of India and State Coordinator, National Register of Citizens, Assam, notes:

> The state's average of exclusion of total number of applicants is 12.15 per cent, surprisingly the border districts and a few others which have seen the maximum increase in population, have average rates of exclusion far below the state average. If the decadal increases in populations for these districts from 1971 to 2011 are juxtaposed against the percentages of exclusion, the pictures are reversed. Border districts have given figures of exclusion which are far below the state average with Dhubri at 8.25 per cent, Karimganj at 8.17 per cent and South Salmara at 6.79 per

cent. The decadal growth rate of population in the border districts of Dhubri, Goalpara, Barpeta, Karimganj, Nagaon and Morigoan, has been between 21 per cent, 24 per cent for decades between 1991-2001 to 2001-2011, against a state average of increase by 18.19 per cent for 1991-2001 and 16.93 per cent in 2001-2011. The exclusions in NRC are totally contrary to this unnatural growth of population in these districts.[24]

The table below brings out the discrepancy:

Sr. No	District	Percentage of applicants excluded from NRC	Decadal Population Growth	
			1991-2001	2001-2011
	Assam	12.15%	18.19%	16.93%
1	Dhubri	8.25%	22.97%	24.40%
2	Goalpara	11.82%	23.03%	22.74%
3	Barpeta	13.69%	19.62%	21.40%
4	Morigaon	14.67%	21.35%	23.39%
5	Nagaon	15.08%	22.6%	22.09%
6	Karimganj	8.17%	21.87%	20.74%

Hazarika further makes the following observation:

Another surprising district is Nalbari where percentage of exclusions is 4.97 per cent, equivalent to that of Jorhat

---

[24] Available at: https://cjp.org.in/wp-content/uploads/2018/08/page-1-17.pdf. Last accessed on 10 April 2020.

at 4.58 per cent. But the decadal growth of population of Nalbari, particularly in the period 1971-1991 was 75.78 per cent and Jorhat was 33.10 per cent as against a state average of 53.26 per cent for the same period, though figures for 1991 till 2011 periods are slightly below the state average. However, the percentage of exclusion in respect of Nalbari is disproportionately low considering that it has an increase of more than 40 per cent above the state average during 1971-1991.

There were several issues with the field verification reports, which were not subject to quality check and adequate digitization, which further led to large-scale indiscriminate inclusion from border areas with faulty documents. For instance, village panchayat secretaries' statements were accepted without verification, as a large number of migrant villages were not even in existence in 1951 or 1971 and were only of recent origin. The Char areas (river islands) where migrants first reside upon entry into India, under the same NRC centre, showed 90 per cent inclusion as opposed to older villages in the mainland. Sensitivity of border districts and migrant-dominated areas, which have continuously objected to and stalled the identification process, were not accounted for. The best example being the stalling of the pilot NRC project in Barpeta in 2010, by attacking and setting fire an officer from the Deputy Commissioner's Office. Based on several such reports in the media highlighting glaring anomalies in the draft NRC, the demand for re-verification and a fair NRC remains as pressing and relevant as it was before.

In 2014, the Supreme Court, delivering a judgement in the

Assam Sanmilita Mahasangha vs Union of India[25] expressed great displeasure at how the UPA and Congress government in Assam were neither implementing the Assam Accord several years after PM Rajiv Gandhi had signed it nor following through on the process of NRC. The Apex Court observed:

> ...precious little has been done by the Union of India and the State of Assam to implement the other parts of the Accord.
>
> The State of Assam has prepared a White Paper on the Foreigners Issue dated 20 October 2012. We propose to extract large portions of this paper only to show that even as on 20 October 2012, very little has been done to implement paragraphs 5(part), 6, 9 and 10 of the Assam Accord.
>
> It will be seen that the number of tribunals set up is abysmally low resulting in an abysmally low number of decisions by these tribunals. What is interesting to know is that whereas almost 1,50,000 persons were deported between 1961 to 1965 under The Immigrants (Expulsion of Assam) Act, 1950, the number of deportations from 1985 till date is stated to be a mere 2,000 odd. Even these deportees are mostly if not all 'push backs' which results in the same deportees coming back post deportation from a border which is completely porous.

Therefore, for the Congress party, which has visibly failed the country on critical aspects of national security, to now question the BJP for taking forward the unfulfilled commitment

---

[25] 'Supreme Court's comments on mishandling of Assam NRC by UPA and Congress government in Assam'. Available at: https://main.sci.gov.in/jonew/judis/42194.pdf. Last accessed on 10 April 2020.

of the late Rajiv Gandhi, is not just ironical but dangerous gamesmanship.

The Central Government, on its part, has not said that the Assam model will be applied throughout the nation. The Assam NRC, which was application-based, put the burden of proof on the individual, in accordance with the Assam Accord, the governing framework, which necessitated stringent provisions. On the contrary, the pan-India NRC, as envisaged, is an enumeration-based process. Creating unnecessary fear and trying to derail the NRC/NPR exercise by highlighting the Assam model is therefore not justified.

International Perspectives

It is now necessary to consider the scenarios regarding citizenship registers or citizenship identity cards in other countries of the world. The Ministry of External Affairs, Government of India, has reached out to all the major countries in the world to make it clear that the CAA and the NRC are internal matters of India and it has also made it clear that it has the support of most of the countries in the world barring a few.[26] Most developed countries in the world maintain registers of their citizens and have provisions for grant of citizenship certificate. In Canada, for example, there is a process whereby one can apply for a citizenship certificate in the appropriate

---

[26] 'India has reached out to countries across the world on CAA, NRC: MEA', *India Today*, New Delhi, 2 January 2020, available at: https://www.indiatoday.in/india/story/india-has-reached-out-to-countries-across-the-world-on-caa-nrc-mea-1633494-2020-01-02. Last accessed on 11 March 2020.

government departments.[27] In the US as well, citizens are granted a citizenship certificate. The entire process is carried out by the US Citizenship and Immigration Services.[28] Even in the United Kingdom (UK), citizenship certificates are granted.[29] Likewise, in India, the certificate of age, nationality and domicile is granted by the state governments. This certificate is popularly known as a 'domicile certificate'. For the purposes of citizenship by registration as well, a certificate is granted. There is, however, no register of citizens maintained in a single database. Hence, a need is felt to maintain such a register in India as well. Under the public international law regime, though arguments may be made against the CAA on certain accounts, there cannot possibly be any argument whatsoever against a process of preparing/updating a register of all the citizens. It is argued that the CAA and NRC exercises would fall foul of Protocol Relating to Status of Refugees, 1967. However, India is not a signatory to this protocol, and hence, there is no question of the CAA/NRC exercise being questioned on that account.

Citizenship Act and Rules: Parliament Is Supreme; Government Has the Power to Frame Rules

Questions have been raised, particularly after some state governments led by the Opposition questioned the Central

---

[27] Available at: https://www.canada.ca/en/immigration-refugees-citizenship/services/canadian-citizenship/proof-citizenship/about.html. Last accessed on 11 March 2020.

[28] Available at: https://my.uscis.gov/exploremyoptions/proof_of_citizenship_us_citizens. Last accessed on 11 March 2020.

[29] Available at: https://www.gov.uk/get-replacement-citizenship-certificate. Last accessed on 11 March 2020.

Government's jurisdiction to decide exclusively on issues of citizenship and frame rules consequently. Article 11 vests the Parliament with express powers, which allows it to 'make any provision with respect to the acquisition and termination of citizenship and all other matters relating to citizenship'. This was also the intent of Dr B.R. Ambedkar, which is reflected in his statements in the Constituent Assembly debate of 10 August 1949:

> The business of laying down a permanent law of citizenship has been left to Parliament, and as Members will see from the wording of Article 6 as I have moved the entire matter regarding citizenship has been left to Parliament to determine by any law that it may deem fit... The effect of Article 6 is this, that Parliament may not only take away citizenship from those who are declared to be citizens on the date of the commencement of this Constitution by the provisions of Article 5 and those that follow, but Parliament may make altogether a new law embodying new principles. That is the first proposition that has to be borne in mind by who will participate in the debate on these articles. They must not understand that the provisions that we are making for citizenship on the date of the commencement of this Constitution are going to be permanent or unalterable. All that we are doing is to decide ad hoc for the time being.

This is the extent of discretion and prerogative vested on the Parliament which explains why matters of expulsion and admission into India and matters relating to citizenship are present in the Union List. It is clear that the history of Articles 5–11 only strengthens the argument that the scope for application of Article 14 in matters of citizenship is limited.

Similarly, the Citizenship (Registration of Citizenship and Issue of National Identity Cards) Rules, 2003, contain the relevant provisions pertaining to the NPR and the NRC. The rules were made by taking recourse to the power conferred upon the Central Government under Section 18 of the Citizenship Act, 1955. It is argued that the Citizenship Rules, 2003, go beyond the mandate of the enabling provision, i.e., Section 18, which reads as follows:

18. Power to make rules—

(1) The Central Government may, by notification in the Official Gazette make rules to carry out the purposes of this Act.
(2) In particular and without prejudice to the generality of the foregoing power, such rules may provide for—
    (a) the registration of anything required or authorized under this Act to be registered, and the conditions and restrictions in regard to such registration; 1[(aa) the form and manner in which a declaration under sub-section (1) of section 4 shall be made];
    (b) the forms to be used and the registers to be maintained under this Act;
    (c) the administration and taking of oaths of allegiance under this Act and the time within which, and the manner in which, such oaths shall be taken and recorded;
    (d) the giving of any notice required or authorized to be given by any person under this Act;

(e) the cancellation of the registration of, and the cancellation and amendment of certificate of naturalisation relating to, persons deprived of citizenship under this Act, and the delivering up of such certificates for those purposes; 2[(ee) the manner and form in which and the authority to whom declarations referred to in clauses (a) and (b) of sub-section (b) of section 6A shall be submitted and other matters connected with such declarations];

(f) the registration at Indian consulates of the births and deaths of persons of any class or description born or dying outside India;

(g) the levy and collection of fees in respect of applications, registrations, declarations and certificates under this Act, in respect of the taking of an oath of allegiance, and in respect of the supply of certified or other copies of documents;

(h) the authority to determine the question of acquisition of citizenship of another country, the procedure to be followed by such authority and rules of evidence relating to such cases;

(i) the procedure to be followed by the committees of inquiry appointed under section 10 and the conferment on such committees of any of the powers, rights and privileges of civil court; 3[(ia) the procedure to be followed in compulsory registration of the citizens of India under sub-section (5) of section 14A];

(j) the manner in which applications for revision may be made and the procedure to be followed by the Central Government in dealing with such applications; and

(k) any other matter which is to be, or may be, prescribed under this Act.

The Citizenship Rules, 2003, deal with the preparation of a population register, a national register of Indian citizens, and also issuance of national identity cards. It is argued that clauses (a) to (k) of sub-section (2) of Section 18 do not contain any reference to such powers being delegated to the Central Government. Thus, it is argued that the Citizenship Rules, 2003, will be ultra vires the parent Act as they travel beyond the mandate Act and the enabling provision in this regard. However, proponents of this argument fail to notice clause (k) of sub-section (2), which mentions 'any other matter which is to be, or may be, prescribed under this Act.' Furthermore, the critics also fail to notice that the power under sub-section (1) confers the power to carry out the purposes of this Act, i.e., the Citizenship Act, 1955 and sub-section (2) begins with the phrase, 'without prejudice to the generality of the foregoing power.' Hence, prima facie, there is nothing in the rules that travels beyond the parent legislation. Moreover, Section 14A provides for the compulsory registration of citizens and issuance of a national identity card. This, therefore, also falls within the purview of the Citizenship Act, for which rules may be made under Section 18. Accordingly, there is nothing in the Citizenship Rules, 2003, which is contrary to or beyond the purview of the Citizenship Act, 2003.

In the next chapter, the very popular argument that the CAA is striking a death blow to the idea of secularism will be addressed.

Is Secularism under Threat?

The consistent and carefully manipulated narrative that has been woven against the CAA is that it is against the idea of secularism, which is a part of the basic structure of the Constitution of India. The word 'secular' was added to the Preamble to the Constitution of India by the infamous 42nd Amendment in 1976. The CAA, it is argued, is contrary to the idea of secularism because it excludes Muslims from its ambit. It is also contended that citizenship on the basis of religion was never contemplated by the Constitution of India and hence, the CAA, which advances citizenship on the basis of affiliation to certain religious groups, is invalid as it travels beyond the mandate of the Constitutional philosophy of not giving citizenship on the basis of religion. What do we do of this argument? At the outset, it is necessary to test the veracity of the claim that citizenship on the basis of religion was never contemplated by the Constitution of India.

Is Citizenship Based on Religion Contrary to the Constitutional Scheme?

Article 5 of the Constitution of India lays down the criteria as to who can be a citizen of India. It reads as follows:

> At the commencement of this Constitution, every person who has his domicile in the territory of India and—

(a) who was born in the territory of India; or (b) either of whose parents was born in the territory of India; or (c) who has been ordinarily resident in the territory of India for not less than five years immediately preceding such commencement, shall be a citizen of India.

Article 6 of the Constitution of India contains a non-obstante clause and thus, it supersedes Article 5. Article 6 reads as follows:

6. Notwithstanding anything in Article 5, a person who has migrated to the territory of India from the territory now included in Pakistan shall be deemed to be a citizen of India at the commencement of this Constitution if— (a) he or either of his parents or any of his grandparents was born in India as defined in the Government of India Act, 1935 (as originally enacted); and (b) (i) in the case where such person has so migrated before the nineteenth day of July, 1948, he has been ordinarily resident in the territory of India since the date of his migration, or (ii) in the case where such person has so migrated on or after the nineteenth day of July, 1948, he has been registered as a citizen of India by an officer appointed in that behalf by the Government of the Dominion of India on an application made by him therefor to such officer before the commencement of this Constitution in the form and manner prescribed by that Government: Provided that no person shall be so registered unless he has been resident in the territory of India for at least six months immediately preceding the date of his application.

What was the reason for this date—19 July 1948—to be chosen? It was chosen because in the first year after India gained Independence, there was a large influx of people from Pakistan and it was presumed that they were largely Hindus and Sikhs. Hence, to give citizenship to such persons, 19 July 1948 was put as a bar. Jawaharlal Nehru had made the following comments upon this issue in the Constituent Assembly debates:

> Our general rule as you will see in regard to these Partition consequences, is that we accept practically without demur or enquiry that great wave of migration which came from Pakistan to India. We accept them as citizens up to sometime in July 1948. It is possible, of course that in the course of that year many wrong persons came over, whom we might not accept as citizens if we examine each one of them; but it is impossible to examine hundreds of thousands of such cases and we accept the whole lot. After July 1948, that is, about a year ago, we put in some kind of enquiry and a magistrate who normally has prima facie evidence will register them; otherwise he will enquire further and ultimately not register or he will reject. Now all these rules naturally apply to Hindus, Muslims and Sikhs or Christians or anybody else. You cannot have rules for Hindus, for Muslims or for Christians only. It is absurd on the face of it; but in effect, we say that we allow the first year's migration and obviously that huge migration was as a migration of Hindus and Sikhs from Pakistan. The others hardly come into the picture at all.[30]

---

[30] Jawaharlal Nehru, Constituent Assembly Debates, Volume 9, Friday, 12 August 1949.

Post-July 1948, several Muslims too wanted to come back to India. A permit system was introduced for such persons. Nehru comments upon this system too. He observed:

> It is possible that later, because of this permit system, some non-Hindus and non-Sikhs came in. How did they come in? How many came in? There are three types of permits, I am told. One is purely a temporary permit for a month or two, and whatever the period may be, a man comes, and he has got to go back during that period. This does not come into the picture. The other type is a permit, not permanent but something like a permanent permit, which does not entitle a man to settle here, but entitles him to come here repeatedly on business. He comes and goes, and he has a continuing permit. I may say that, of course, does not come into the picture. The third type of permit is a permit given to a person to come here for permanent stay, that is, return to India and settle down here. Now, in the case of all these permits, a great deal of care has been taken in the past before issuing them. In the case of those permits which are meant for permanent return to India and settling here again, a very great deal of care has been taken. The local officials of the place where the man came from and where he wants to go back are addressed; the local government is addressed, and it is only when sufficient reason is found by the local officials and the local Government that our High Commissioner in Karachi or Lahore, as the case may be, issues that kind of permit.[31]

---

[31] ibid.

It appears that there was an apprehension that since the wave of Muslims coming back to India was huge, a large number of permits will be issued, and communal tensions would again erupt. Hence, a member of the Constituent Assembly questioned Nehru as to how many such permits were issued, to which Nehru replied that only about 2,000 to 3,000 permits were issued.[32] The correspondences between our leaders also reflect that India was not keen to rehabilitate the Muslim refugees against the interests of the non-Muslim refugees. Several eminent scholars have attacked the CAA by claiming that it is against secularism and that it is inherently communal. Would they also assign the same intent to the apprehensions about issuing permits to Muslim migrants in the aftermath of the Partition? Some scholars have recently pointed out that on examination of the background of enactment of the citizenship provisions, it is noticed that they do not have secular origins.[33]

The practical difficulty in rehabilitating Muslims who had come back to India from Pakistan was a very serious one since Hindus who came to India from Pakistan had occupied the houses of the Muslims who left India. The question of the titles of these properties would then creep up. In light of this, certain apprehensions were also raised by the members of the Constituent Assembly. Sardar Hukum Singh said:

---

[32] Shri Gopikrishna Vijayvargiya, Constituent Assembly Debates, Volume 9, Friday, 12 August 1949.

[33] Dr Abhinav Chandrachud, 'Secularism and the Citizenship Amendment Act', Paper Presentation (February 2020), Victoria, University of Wellington, available at: https://papers.ssrn.com/sol3/papers.cfm?abstract_id=3513828. Last accessed on 6 March 2020.

> Sir, we have been told that the Muslims, who left their property here and have come back, retain their titles to the property that was left here, and when they come back, it is simple justice to return them that property. Government cannot do anything else. This is very good. I want to know from the honourable Mover whether according to his logic, we, who have come from Pakistan and left our properties there, also retain our titles to those properties. Can he suggest us some court or tribunal before whom we can go and place those title deeds to get justice that is being accorded to these people here by this proviso?[34]

Dr P.S. Deshmukh, another honourable member, questioned on the same lines:

> May I ask a question? The real question which my Friend intended to ask was, to what extent there is reciprocity so far as admission of non-Muslims in the Pakistan areas was concerned, and I do not think any satisfactory answer was given to that question. What we want to know is to what extent has the Honourable Minister found the Pakistan Government reciprocating to the ideas and ideals that we hold, and propagate and the policies that we adopt?[35]

To which N. Gopalaswami Iyengar confessed that the response from Pakistan had not been satisfactory. In light of enactment

---

[34] Sardar Hukum Singh, Constituent Assembly Debates, Volume 9, Friday, 12 August, 1949.
[35] Dr P.S. Deshmukh, Constituent Assembly Debates, Volume 9, Friday, 12 August 1949.

of Article 6, the cut-off date, and in light of the debates in the Constituent Assembly and circumstances prevalent after Partition, it would be difficult to say that the citizenship provisions in the Constitution of India were truly secular. Pandit Thakur Das Bhargava, while commenting upon the citizenship provisions contained in the Constitution of India, observed:

> Our provisions relating to citizenship are very generous and they extend citizenship not only to persons having domicile in India but also to five or six millions of persons who having been uprooted from Pakistan have migrated to India. Even the persons who had migrated to Pakistan but have again returned back to India under a permit for resettlement have been made citizens of India. No doubt in their case, legally we should have waited for five years but I think it matters little that they had left India, and if they want to resettle here we can give them the citizenship of our State, for originally they had their domicile in India.[36]

It is therefore clear that doubts were expressed even at the time of the Constituent Assembly debates about who came and who left for what reasons, and there is a serious doubt as to the secular origins of the Constitution's citizenship provisions. Hence, it cannot be argued that since the Constitution of India does not contemplate citizenship on the basis of religion, the CAA would be invalid on that count alone. The origins of the present-day India are in the religious nature of the Partition of

---

[36] Pandit Thakur Das Bhargava, Constituent Assembly Debates, Volume 11, Friday, 18 November 1949.

India, and the segregation—both out of free will and forced—was influenced by the nature of it.

Before moving on from the discussion in this section, it is necessary to note that secularism was not originally a part of the Constitution of India. K.M. Munshi, speaking against an amendment, which sought to include the words 'secular', 'federal' and 'socialist', to the draft Constitution moved by K.T. Shah on 15 November 1948, said:

> A secular state is not without God. It is not a state which has resolved to uproot religion… it is not a state which denies religious faith in the country.[37]

Loknath Mishra, another honourable member, was even more trenchant in his observation:

> Gradually it seems to me that our 'secular state' is a slippery phrase, a device to by-pass the ancient culture of the land. The absurdity of this position is now manifest in articles 19 to 22 of the Draft Constitution. Do we really believe that religion can be divorced from life, or is it our belief that in the midst of many religions we cannot decide which one to accept? If religion is beyond the ken of our State, let us clearly say so and delete all reference to rights relating to religion. If we find it necessary, let us be brave enough and say what it should be.[38]

Dr Ambedkar, while debating the inclusion of the word 'secular' in the Constitution, made the following statement:

---

[37] Shri K.M. Munshi, Constituent Assembly Debates, Volume 7, 6 December 1948.
[38] Shri Loknath Mishra, Constituent Assembly Debates, Volume 7, 6 December 1948.

What should be the policy of the State, how the Society should be organised in its social and economic side are matters which must be decided by the people themselves according to time and circumstances. It cannot be laid down in the Constitution itself because that is destroying democracy altogether.

The question that may, however, be raised is: although the secular origins of the Constitution can be doubted, but since secularism is now part of the basic structure, is the CAA not violative of the said principle and hence constitutionally invalid?

Admittedly, the Supreme Court of India has held that secularism forms part of the basic structure of the Constitution of India. In the case of State of Karnataka vs Dr Praveen Togadia,[39] the Court explained the meaning of the term 'secularism':

> Secularism means that the State should have no religion of its own, and each person, whatever his religion, must get an assurance from the State that he has the protection of law, freely to profess, practice and propagate his religion and freedom of conscience.

The Supreme Court then made a reference to the case of S.R. Bommai vs Union of India[40] and reiterated that secularism is a part of the fundamental law and an unalienable segment of the basic structure of the Constitution of India. Another interesting precedent in this regard is the case of Santosh

---

[39] (2004) 4 SCC 684.
[40] (1994) 3 SCC 1.

Kumar vs The Secretary, MHRD[41] wherein the inclusion of only Sanskrit and not Arabic and Persian as an elective subject was challenged before the Apex Court as being violative of secularism. The court reiterated that secularism is part of the basic structure of the Constitution of India but held that it could not find fault with the inclusion of only Sanskrit as an elective subject and thus rejected the challenge.

It is necessary, at this stage, to make a note about arguments claiming that the CAA is against the secular nature of India. The most popular argument in this regard, and which has been taken note of earlier in this chapter, is that Muslims are excluded from the CAA and therefore this is against secular principles. Further, it is argued that exclusion of groups such as atheists, agnostics and others also fall foul of the concept of secularism. Moreover, it is pointed out that the law does not include Jews and Parsis from Iran and also that it does not include the Sri Lankan Tamils. These are the significant arguments that have been made against the CAA.

It is to be first ascertained whether the CAA legislation undermines the basic structure of the Constitution. It is necessary to emphatically state that the CAA does not violate the principle of secularism. However, the position in Indian constitutional jurisprudence is that parliamentary legislation is challenged on the anvil of violation of fundamental rights and constitutional amendments are challenged on the anvil of violation of the basic structure. The CAA is a parliamentary legislation and not a constitutional amendment. Secularism, as a principle, is not a fundamental right but, undoubtedly, a part of the basic structure of the Constitution of India. The

---

[41] (1994) 6 SCC 579.

basic structure theory was developed by the Supreme Court of India in Kesavananda Bharati vs State of Kerala[42] as a tool for the judiciary to consider the constitutional validity of amendments to the Constitution. Article 13 of the Constitution of India, as interpreted by the courts, makes it clear that laws that violate fundamental rights shall be void to that extent and the courts shall have the power to strike down laws that violate the fundamental rights. As noted above, the CAA is a law made by the Parliament. It is not an amendment to the Constitution. Thus, its constitutional validity will have to be determined on the grounds that it violates the fundamental rights of citizens and not on the basis of it being a threat to the basic structure of the Constitution.

As made clear by the Apex Court in numerous cases, the constitutional amendments can be tested on the anvil of the basic structure. Hence, it is wrong to say that the CAA violates the basic structure of the Constitution of India and is liable to be struck down as unconstitutional. It may, however, be argued that laws that violate the basic structure would definitely violate some fundamental rights. Even if this is taken to be true, the law made by the Parliament or state legislatures would have to be challenged on the grounds that they violated one or some of the fundamental rights guaranteed under the Constitution. The argument that the CAA is against the principle of secularism can thus be made by making reference to Article 14 of the Constitution of India, which is the equality clause of the Constitution.

---

[42] (1973) 4 SCC 225.

Does CAA Violate Article 14?

In the early days after the Constitution was accepted, the principle applied by the Supreme Court to test the validity of laws and whether they violated Article 14 was that of reasonable classification.[43] Thus, if the state could show that the classification was based on an intelligible differentia and hence a reasonable classification, then the classification would be held to be valid and the analysis on the anvil of Article 14 would end there. However, subsequently, some doubts were raised as to the efficacy of the reasonable classification test. In the State of West Bengal vs Anwar Ali Sarkar,[44] for example, Justice Vivian Bose tried to lay the foundations for a new test. He noted that the approach of the courts could not be 'doctrinaire' while considering the constitutional validity of laws on the anvil of Article 14. While laying down a new test, he observed as follows:

> What I am concerned to see is not whether there is absolute equality in any academical sense of the term but whether the collective conscience of a sovereign democratic republic can regard the impugned law, contrasted with the ordinary law of the land, as the sort of substantially equal treatment which men of resolute minds and unbiased views can regard as right and proper in a democracy of the kind we have proclaimed ourselves to be. Such views must take into consideration the practical necessities of government, the right to alter the laws and many other facts, but in the forefront must

---

[43] Chiranjit Lal Chowdhury vs Union of India, AIR 1951 SC 41.
[44] AIR 1952 SC 75.

> remain the freedom of the individual from unjust and unequal treatment, unequal in the broad sense in which a democracy would view it. In my opinion, 'law' as used in Article 14 does not mean the 'legal precepts which are actually recognised and applied in the tribunals of a given time and place' but 'the more general body of doctrine and tradition from which those precepts are chiefly drawn, and by which we criticise, them.'

Thus, it can be seen that if a law shook the 'collective conscience of a sovereign democratic republic', it could be regarded as invalid and ultra vires of Article 14. Subsequent to this, for some years, the reasonable classification test came to be invoked again and again by the Apex Court. However, in the 1970s and 1980s, the foundations for the test of 'arbitrariness' were laid. In E.P. Royappa vs State of Tamil Nadu,[45] Justice Bhagwati famously observed that equality is antithetic to arbitrariness. He further went on to virtually lay down the test of arbitrariness as a ground to strike down the laws that he considered violated Article 14 by observing the following:

> Equality is a dynamic concept with many aspects and dimensions, and it cannot be 'cribbed cabined and confined' within traditional and doctrinaire limits. From a positivistic point of view, equality is antithetic to arbitrariness. In fact, equality and arbitrariness are sworn enemies; one belongs to the rule of law in a republic while the other, to the whim and caprice of an absolute monarch. Where an act is arbitrary it is implicit in it that it is unequal both according to political

---

[45] AIR 1974 SC 555.

logic and constitutional law and is therefore violative of Article 14, and if it affects any matter relating to public employment, it is also violative of Article 16. Articles 14 and 16 strike at arbitrariness in State action and ensure fairness and equality of treatment. They require that State action must be based on relevant principles applicable alike to all similarly situate and it must not be guided by any extraneous or irrelevant considerations because that would be denial of equality. Where the operative reason for State action, as distinguished from motive inducing from the antechamber of the mind, is not legitimate and relevant but is extraneous and outside the area of permissible considerations, it would amount to mala fide exercise of power and that is hit by Articles 14 and 16.[46]

Justice Bhagwati noted that reasonable classification was not a paraphrase of equality and that it was only one of the means whereby a judge could decide whether there was an element of arbitrariness or not.

Finally, in the case of Shayara Bano vs Union of India,[47] Justice Nariman, referring to the entire jurisprudential growth of Article 14, reached the conclusion that 'manifest arbitrariness' is a ground to strike down laws as being violative of Article 14. This test was applied later in the case of Navtej Singh Johar vs Union of India[48] and in subsequent judgements as well. However, it is to be noted that in no ruling on Article 14 has the Court held that the test of reasonable classification is no more

---

[46] (1981) 1 SCC 722.
[47] (2017) 9 SCC 1.
[48] (2018) 10 SCC 1.

a sound test. Now that the jurisprudential development in this regard has been highlighted, we will have to consider whether the CAA is manifestly arbitrary and thus violative of Article 14. The CAA caters to the interests of the religious minorities in Pakistan, Bangladesh and Afghanistan. Such a classification would not be bad simply because it excludes some other countries or that it excludes other oppressed groups that face oppression on other grounds. In State of Madhya Pradesh vs Bhopal Sugar Industries,[49] the Apex Court observed as follows:

> The Legislature has always the power to make special laws to attain particular objects and for that purpose has authority to select or classify persons, objects or transactions upon which the law is intended to operate. Differential treatment becomes unlawful only when it is arbitrary or not supported by a rational relation with the object of the statute... Where application of unequal laws is reasonably justified for historical reasons, a geographical classification founded on those historical reasons would be upheld.

It is also contended that 'religion' cannot be a reasonable basis for classification. However, the Apex Court, in the case of Mahant Moti Das vs S.P. Sahi[50] has in fact held that religion could also be a reasonable basis for classification. The CAA can be compared to the Lautenberg Amendment, 1989, of the US that gives refugee status and eventually citizenship to a set of minorities from three countries. The Lautenberg-Specter Amendment, 2004, recognized that some refugees like

---

[49] (1964) 6 SCR 846.
[50] AIR 1959 SC 942.

the Jews, Christians and the Baha'is, belonging to specific religions and from specific countries could be identified as historically persecuted groups. The United States Commission on International Religious Freedom (USCIRF), which recently criticized the Modi government on the CAA, had in fact spoken in favour of the Lautenberg–Specter Amendment.[51]

As regards Article 14, it cannot be said that there is no material on record which has enabled the State to reach the conclusion that members of the religious groups mentioned in the CAA are facing religious persecution in the three countries mentioned therein. The three countries are the ones that have Islam as the dominant religion. There is ample evidence of religious persecution upon which the State will place reliance during the hearing of the CAA petitions. Hence, the ground that this entire exercise is arbitrary cannot be raised. It also needs to be appreciated that 'religion' is not the predominant factor to be considered in this debate. The predominant factor is probability of facing religious persecution. It is this probability that qualifies religion.

Another relevant argument in this regard is that our Constitution has granted ample protection to minorities in India. Hence, if the State tries to take any measures to protect religious minorities in neighbouring states, such an action cannot be frowned upon. The 'degree of harm' test also needs to be looked at in this context. In Chiranjit Lal Chowdhury vs The Union of India and Others,[52] the Court had held that the

---

[51] Available at: https://economictimes.indiatimes.com/news/politics-and-nation/caa-has-corollary-in-us-lautenberg-amendment/articleshow/73347361.cms?from=mdr. Last accessed on 13 March 2020.
[52] AIR 1951 SC 41.

discretion of the State needs to be protected. It observed as follows:

> It is also true that the class of persons to whom a law is made applicable may be large or small, and the degree of harm which has prompted the enactment of a particular law is a matter within the discretion of the law-makers. It is not the province of the Court to canvass the legislative judgement in such matters.

There is also another way of looking at this entire debate. The most significant amendment brought in by the CAA is the insertion of a proviso to the definition of 'illegal migrant'. Thus, 'illegal migrants' constitute an entire class and some of them, by the operation of the proviso, cannot be classified as illegal migrants. The Supreme Court, in the case of General Manager, Uttaranchal Jal Sansthan vs Laxmi Devi[53] has held that 'Equality clause cannot be applied in cases where it arises out of illegality.' All those who are going to be affected by the CAA are 'illegal migrants'. Hence, being illegal migrants, they have committed an illegality. It follows that 'illegal migrants' cannot constitute an entire class in order to claim 'equality' and, consequentially, the fundamental right under Article 14. The equality clause cannot, therefore, be invoked since it is emanating from an existing illegality. It would thus not be correct to say that the word 'person' in Article 14 would also include illegal migrants.

The secularism argument is further buttressed by referring to the cause of the Jews from Pakistan, the minority Muslim groups in Pakistan, Parsees from Iran, etc. These arguments

---

[53] (2009) 7 SCC 205.

can also be easily addressed. Firstly, there has to be extrinsic evidence to suggest that members from these communities have also fled those countries and residing illegally in India for the last five years or more. If a significant number of people belonging to these groups have not been residing in India, then the law would justifiably not make any provision for them.

Questions have been raised regarding the non-inclusion of minorities from within the larger Muslim community in Pakistan, such as the Shias and Ahmadiyyas. At the outset, it needs to be stated that Pakistan is an Islamic country, and hence there cannot be institutionalized oppression against 'Muslims' as a broad religious group. If the sects/minorities within this group are also to be considered, then the question arises: where do we stop? There could be further subclasses within the subclasses, *reductio ad absurdum*. For example, the Shia population in Pakistan is 10–15 per cent[54] (therefore, numbering about 21 million to 31.5 million people). Would they all be considered religiously persecuted? The constitutionality of CAA therefore cannot be considered on this ground. Pakistan being an Islamic Republic, non-inclusion of Muslims, of whatever Muslim denomination, cannot therefore be considered unreasonable or arbitrary.

The question regarding Jews, Baha'is, and others like atheists can also be addressed easily. Keeping the question of the constitutional validity of the CAA apart, the Court may, in such cases, say to the activist petitioners that if any such person belonging to such groups approaches the

---

[54] Available at: https://www.pewresearch.org/wp-content/uploads/sites/7/2009/10/Shiarange.pdf. Last accessed 10 April 2020.

Supreme Court, then the Court would consider his or her case. Assuming that such a person indeed appears before the Court, then the Court may also invoke Article 142 of the Constitution of India, which is the power of the Apex Court to do complete justice in a matter and advance citizenship status to such a person. The constitutional validity of the CAA cannot thus be challenged on these grounds alone. Secondly, while considering the validity of the CAA under Article 14 and secularism, the Court will not remain oblivious of the existence of Article 11, which reads as follows:

> Parliament to regulate the right of citizenship by law— Nothing in the foregoing provisions of this Part shall derogate from the power of Parliament to make any provision with respect to the acquisition and termination of citizenship and all other matters relating to citizenship.

This constitutional provision is a part of the chapter that contains the provisions relating to citizenship and emerges from all the provisions of citizenship contained in the Constitution. This provision recognizes the sovereign power of the State to make any law for the acquisition or termination of citizenship. On a reference to this provision and to the theory that the power of the State in this sphere is unfettered, the Court would dismiss the challenge to the validity of the CAA. It is also clearly pointed out that the CAA has nothing to do with the status of existing citizens of India and since it advances the interests of the minorities of the three neighbouring countries, it cannot on that count be regarded as un-secular and ultra vires the Constitution of India.

It has to be reiterated that Pakistan, Afghanistan and

Bangladesh are Islamic republics. The very title to the Constitution of Pakistan is 'The Constitution of the Islamic Republic of Pakistan'. The Afghanistan Constitution begins with the phrase, 'In the name of Allah, the Most Beneficent, the Most Merciful.' Bangladesh was founded on secular credentials, but the secularism principle was removed in 1977 by the 5th Amendment to its constitution. Bangladesh declared Islam as the state religion in 1988, and Bangladesh's High Court upheld Islam as the state religion in 2016.

India, unlike its neighbours, is a secular state in the sense that it does not have a state religion. This fact does not erase India's past as the cradle of Hindu civilization, which, many have eloquently argued, makes it inherently secular. How so? It is because unlike monopolist and monotheistic religions that swear by one book, and make claims to the 'Truth', one cannot remain oblivious of the remarkable pronouncement in the Rig Veda (1:164:46): '*Ekam Sat Viprah Bahudha Vadanti*, which means there is one truth and the great saints and rishis of this land call it differently—Indra, Mitra, Varuna, Agni, etc. This idea is enshrined in our civilizational values stretching back millennia, making us not just tolerant of differing ideologies and worldviews but celebrating and debating them.

As noted earlier in this chapter, the word 'secular' was not originally included in the Constitution of India. It was added by the 42nd Amendment to the Constitution. Nirmala Sitharaman, the current finance minister, had in 2013, succinctly commented about it:

> It is ironical that the Congress party brought in changes in the basic structure of our Constitution when, originally, after due discussions, the intention of our lawmakers

was not to have the words 'socialist' and 'secular'. And even when they imposed these terms, through the 42nd Amendment, they lacked clarity and commitment to their spoken words. Today, as we discuss this issue in a globally liberalized world, one wonders what is 'socialist' about the way we define ourselves. A welfare state need not necessarily be a socialist state. By the same measure, wasn't India secular before the 42nd Amendment?[55]

Writing his opinion in Dr M. Ismail Faruqui vs Union of India,[56] Justice Bharucha observed:

> Hinduism is a tolerant faith. It is that tolerance that has enabled Islam, Christianity, Zoroastrianism, Judaism, Buddhism, Jainism and Sikhism to find shelter and support upon this land.

We cannot ignore the fact that the original Constitution of India, as illustrated by Nandalal Bose, the famous artist from Bengal, had rich depictions of India's ancient cultural heritage and traditions. It contains pictures of Lord Nataraja, Ganganayan by Bhagirath, Lord Ram's victory over Lanka, illustrations of the Vedic life of India, Nalanda University, Guru Gobind Singh, Chhatrapati Shivaji Maharaj, Rani Jhansi, Maharana Pratap, Kabir Das, and even the Himalayas. The chapter on Fundamental Rights contains pictures of Lord Ram returning with Lakshman and Sita from Lanka to Ayodhya, and the chapter on the Directive Principles of State Policy depicts Lord Krishna's great *upadesh*

---

[55] Nirmala Sitharaman, 'Secularism and the Constitution of India'. *The Asian Age*, August 2013.
[56] (1994) 6 SCC 360.

(teaching) from the Bhagavad Gita.[57] If this is the spirit of India, as enshrined in the original Constitution of India, then how can it ever be questioned on its commitment to secularism?

It is imperative to note that the CAA is also in the best interests of a large majority of Dalits who have also fled Pakistan due to persecution. Pakistan did not permit Scheduled Castes (SCs) populations to migrate to India in its early years. Now that the CAA is in place, Dalits would be able to have a safe haven in India. The critics of CAA will have to answer why they are against the interests of Dalits.

In the next chapter, we will look at what leaders such as Jawaharlal Nehru, Mahatma Gandhi and Sardar Patel said about matters of state and religion, and the status of Hindu and Sikh refugees.

---

[57] Available at: https://hinduexistence.org/2014/01/26/hindu-elements-in-indian-constitution/. Last accessed on 4 February 2020.

Why the Debate?

Since the passage of the CAA in December 2019, the country has seen widespread agitations led and instigated by several political and religious groups throughout the country. The agitation-planners' agenda is clear: generate fear in the minds of the Muslims of the country, stoke anger among the youth and the impressionable, and organize marches and sit-ins that will bring life to a standstill in many localities. The fear that had been incited among Muslims is that they will be gradually reduced to second-class citizens and subsequently thrown out of the country. The videos of the agitations and interviews of gullible individuals who joined the protests make this very clear. It is therefore necessary to ascertain the intention behind these agitations and address the specious and provocative arguments being made against the CAA.

A Step towards Hindu Rashtra?

Several political leaders as well as prejudiced academics, media commentators and activists have repeatedly and provocatively asserted that the CAA is nothing but a step taken towards achieving the goal of 'Hindu Rashtra'. Such statements are in the public domain. Our purpose here is neither to respond to their diatribes on 'Hindu Rashtra', nor to enlighten readers/

citizens about what Hindutva or Hindu Rashtra really means and how the concept of Hindu Rashtra is not inimical to the concept of secularism. That debate can be had at a different time, at an appropriate place. However, it is necessary to point out that the political rivals of the BJP fail to notice the basic difference between the concept of 'nation' and the concept of 'state'. The literal translation of the word 'rashtra' is 'nation' and not 'state'. The Rashtriya Swayamsevak Sangh (RSS) has always maintained that India is and has always been a Hindu Rashtra. There is no need to declare it to be so by law. Moreover, the definition of the word 'Hindu', which was propounded by Veer Savarkar, is also an inclusive one. This brief reference is made only for the purpose of pointing out that the Opposition and the 'mainstream' narrative builders are missing a point. It is wrong to say that this is a step towards 'Hindu Rashtra'. It is a step towards a policy that rejects appeasement politics, pandering to particular groups, and assuring the rights of those minorities who are facing religious persecution at the hands of extremists, rogue states and agents provocateurs. It is mischievous, if not criminal, to argue that religious minorities in Pakistan, Afghanistan and Bangladesh are not facing religious persecution. It is a part of Indian ethos to welcome persecuted people. The Citizenship (Amendment) Bill (CAB) was formulated, and the CAA enacted in keeping with the great ethos of India.

The Hindu Rashtra argument falls apart for another very important reason: the CAA is not a law that protects only Hindu minorities from the three neighbouring countries, but it is also a conscious attempt to protect the interests of other persecuted groups, including Christians, Buddhists, Jains and Sikhs. Non-inclusion of Muslim groups, as we pointed out in the earlier section, is a logical and valid stance in this context. Minorities among Muslims do not constitute a separate group. They are a subgroup within a larger group. The religions mentioned in the CAA are groups in themselves. The classification is between the larger groups. Moreover, attributing motives to the state would be of no avail while testing the validity of the CAA. The least that is expected of the anti-CAA crusaders is that they present an honest account of history and also of the conflicting ideologies that has brought this situation to a pass.

Biased and Dishonest Narratives

Since the BJP came back to power in 2019, backed by a strong, historic and unprecedented mandate, it has taken bold and necessary moves to change the dynamics in the country. After the abrogation of Article 370 and the promulgation of the Jammu and Kashmir Reorganisation Act, 2019, the Modi government was in a strong position, and there was hearty backing of that action by a vast majority of people in the country, including many Opposition leaders. After the Supreme Court passed its judgement on the Ayodhya Ram Mandir issue, frustration grew among Opposition parties and anti-BJP activists. Therefore, an attempt was made to stoke discontent among Muslims. After the passage of the CAA, the Opposition saw an opportunity to reverse the trend and destabilize the government. Hence, the protests. Every attempt was made to show the government in a bad light and to provoke communal tensions. They have been largely successful in their attempt, garnering strength from a variety of foreign sources too. An attempt was also made to garner sympathy for the Muslims by using the victim card. A systematic and coordinated attempt was made to show

Hindus in a bad light. Sections of the international media and the Left/Marxist lobby in the Indian media left no stone unturned in painting the 2019 elections as a manifestation of communal hatred and marginalizing minorities.

When the preparation for the 2019 elections began, *The New York Times* published an article titled, 'Under Modi, a Hindu Nationalist surge has further divided India.'[58] This is but one among hundreds of examples that show how the international media tried to fashion an anti-Hindu, anti-BJP, anti-Modi narrative. The attempts to spread fear among the minds of Muslims and to make Hindus feel apologetic were rampant. If we were to analyse *The New York Times*'s article, the title of the article itself leads one to believe that India is divided, and that it is the Hindu nationalists who have divided India. Then they accuse Modi, the prime minister who enjoys the support of more than half the House, as responsible for all this. It is also necessary to note that the article does not make any attempt to define Hindu nationalism. Instead, what it does is to start with an interview of a member of the Muslim community expressing his fears. The article mentions that people are afraid to walk alone on the streets at night. The reporters then assert 'Hindu lynch mobs' began to pop up across the Indian landscape, killing Muslims and people from the lower castes, and that these mobs often got away. It is easy to notice that the article identifies the lynch mobs as 'Hindu lynch mobs'. Showcasing some criminals as 'Hindus' is something that the narrative-builders have done very

---

[58] Jeffrey Gettleman, Kai Schultz, Suhasini Raj and Hari Kumar, 'Under Modi, a Hindu Nationalist surge has further divided India,' *The New York Times*, 11 April 2019, available at: https://www.nytimes.com/2019/04/11/world/asia/modi-india-elections.html. Last accessed on 10 March 2020.

efficiently. The nature, purpose and intent of the article are thus clear and nothing more needs to be said about the goals of the reporters and the editors of this newspaper that claims to be the 'newspaper of record'. This is but one article in a series of such lopsided, contemptible and provocative pieces of 'reporting' from *The New York Times*'s New Delhi stable of correspondents and reporters. There are several other such reports across print and electronic media, repeatedly painting Hindus in dark colours and completely absolving everyone else of all misdeeds, ill-intent and anti-Hindu bigotry. According to these media sources, if not for Hindus, India would be a happy, peaceful and prosperous country where religious harmony would prevail, and India would be a 'secular' heaven.

These newspapers and magazines as well as radio and television reports have consistently and deliberately charged Hindus with hate crimes against Muslims, Dalits, Adivasis, women, etc. These narratives, whether in newspaper articles, activist groups' studies, or so-called research by compromised academics, also try to paint a picture that no crimes are committed by Muslims, Christians and others against Hindus. We very well know the trajectory and the beginnings of such sprees of violence in India, and how political mischief-makers, sleeper cells and international actors have been meddling in India's affairs seeking to destabilize the country. After the enactment of the CAA, the number of these articles, essays and studies has risen astronomically. Unfortunately, both readers and viewers in India and around the world have fallen prey to these ill-motivated narratives. When Yakub Memon, a terrorist who was sentenced to death for his role in the 1993 bomb blasts that rocked Mumbai, was ultimately executed, a huge mob had gathered for his funeral. His funeral procession from

Mahim to Marine Lines in Mumbai saw a huge crowd.[59] This is but one example where a terrorist who was sentenced to death for the brutal murder of hundreds of the country's citizens got 'secular' sympathy. Western narrative-builders and their well-paid Indian collaborators and enablers have, of course, conveniently ignored every damning fact about mischief, crime and discrimination by non-Hindus.

Protests or Riots? The Role Played by Narrative-Builders

The peaceful protests against the CAA, on several occasions, turned into riots, for which, obviously, a desperate attempt was made to show that the Central Government was squarely responsible. When the protests turned violent, the job of the narrative-builders began. They once again tried to show that Muslims were the targets and the ones who suffered despite the fact that such protests were Muslim-led or inspired rioters who had gone berserk. Again, an attempt was desperately made to show Hindus in a bad light.

An article by Mukul Kesavan, published in *The Guardian*, is another example of anti-Hindu sentiment peddled as expert narrative. Kesavan writes:

> The riots have been driven by a ruling party intent on painting its largely peaceful opponents as seditious sectarians.

---

[59] 'Huge crowd at Yakub Memon's funeral driven by Dawood Ibrahim's diktat?' *DNA India*, 8 August 2015, available at: https://www.dnaindia.com/india/report-huge-crowd-at-yakub-memon-s-funeral-driven-by-dawood-ibrahim-s-diktat-2112238. Last accessed on 10 March 2020.

This clearly biased and agenda-driven article further reads:

> The time-honoured convention for reporting on communal violence in India is to not name names. In news reports it is always 'violent members of one religious community' attacking violent members of another. This anonymising ritual has the distorting effect of turning unequal violence into a symmetrical tug of war. It is important, then, to specify that the places of worship vandalised were two mosques and a Sufi shrine, that the majority of identified dead people were Muslims, that the thugs frisking reporters, confiscating their phones and beating them up were in every instance Hindu supremacist goons, and that the shops and homes burned nearly always belonged to Muslims.[60]

Without any evidence, the writer accuses 'Hindu supremacist goons' as the perpetrators of violence. It is necessary to state here that all across the media and on the Internet, several videos have surfaced which have shown groups of men, identified as Muslim mobs, pelting stones. Truckloads of bricks, stones and projectiles were delivered over weeks to Muslim-majority localities, which were then used in deadly assault against the police and the ordinary public.[61] When faced with this, Kesavan again asserts without evidence:

---

[60] Mukul Kesavan, 'Anti-Muslim violence in Delhi serves Modi well,' *The Guardian*, 26 February 2020, available at: https://www.theguardian.com/commentisfree/2020/feb/26/violence-delhi-modi-project-bjp-citizenship-law. Last accessed on 18 March 2020.

[61] Available at: https://www.indiatoday.in/india/story/were-delhi-riots-pre-planned-police-point-to-evidence-tumbling-now-1650914-2020-02-28. Last accessed on 10 April 2020.

There were occasions when Muslims burned cars, there is video evidence of a man identified as Muslim who fired a gun, and several instances of stone-throwing by Muslims. But the organising impresarios of this devastation were local politicians affiliated to the Bharatiya Janata Party (BJP), India's ruling party. They made the incendiary speeches that triggered the violence.

Thus, no matter which religious group participates in the violence, as per the author's 'wisdom' and conjecture, it is the BJP leaders who are responsible!

Al Jazeera took note of some random gatherings in US cities against the so-called 'anti-Muslim' violence. The report notes that, 'Violence erupted in the Indian capital on Monday, leading to a three-day-long rampage, with Hindu mobs attacking Muslim homes, shops and mosques.'[62] This report too, which is an unabashedly anti-Hindu and anti-BJP narrative, holds 'Hindu mobs' squarely responsible for the riots. Another article published in *The Nation* by Fahad Shah also begins with a story of a Muslim labourer who was lynched by a 'Hindu mob'.[63] Beginning articles by highlighting such individual cases and then portraying the entire 'right wing' and the 'Hindu' as a whole in a very bad light, nationally and internationally, is the typical modus operandi of these thoroughly biased narrative-builders.

---

[62] Samira Sadeque, 'Hundreds rally in US cities against Anti-Muslim violence in Delhi,' *Al Jazeera*, 1 March 2020, available at: https://www.aljazeera.com/news/2020/02/hundreds-rally-cities-anti-muslim-violence-delhi-200229223719285.html. Last accessed on 10 March 2020.

[63] Fahad Shah, 'The Government has done this: Inside India's Muslim pogrom,' *The Nation*, 5 March 2020, available at: https://www.thenation.com/article/world/india-delhi-violence/. Last accessed on 10 March 2020.

The BBC has not been far behind in publishing such anti-Hindu, anti-BJP narratives. One such article needs to be taken note of. In the article, 'Why Delhi violence has echoes of the Gujarat riots,' Soutik Biswas has tried to paint a similar picture. He begins his reporting by observing as follows:

> What began as small clashes between supporters and opponents of a controversial citizenship law quickly escalated into full-blown religious riots between Hindus and Muslims, in congested working class neighbourhoods on the fringes of the sprawling capital. Armed Hindu mobs rioted with impunity as the police appeared to look the other way. Mosques and homes and shops of Muslims were attacked, sometimes allegedly with the police in tow. Journalists covering the violence were stopped by the Hindu rioters and asked about their religion. Videos and pictures emerged of the mob forcing wounded Muslim men to recite the national anthem, and mercilessly beating up a young Muslim man. Panicky Muslims began leaving mixed neighbourhoods.[64]

There are several such articles that have painted a picture that only Muslims are the victims of mob violence perpetrated by Hindus. These articles do not deserve to be countered much on the merits of their claims. However, it is necessary to point out some facts about the Delhi riots engineered by others against the CAA and unpack the anti-Hindu narrative for their ill-intent, if not provocative mischief. At this juncture, it is necessary to point out the conduct of these journalists, columnists, academics and activists and how their conduct and their

---

[64] Available at: https://www.bbc.com/news/world-asia-india-51641516.

product are deplorable and deserve to be condemned. These biased and provocative writing with screaming headlines that further propelled and fueled the riots are against the 'Norms of Journalistic Conduct' of the Press Council of India. These standards contain a specific clause that deals with covering of communal disputes and violence. It reads as follows:

> 20 (i) News, views or comments relating to communal or religious disputes/clashes shall be published after proper verification of facts and presented with due caution and restraint in a manner which is conducive to the creation of an atmosphere congenial to communal harmony, amity and peace. Sensational, provocative and alarming headlines are to be avoided. Acts of communal violence or vandalism shall be reported in a manner as may not undermine the people's confidence in the law and order machinery of the State. Giving community-wise figures of the victims of communal riot, or writing about the incident in a style which is likely to inflame passions, aggravate the tension, or accentuate the strained relations between the communities/religious groups concerned, or which has a potential to exacerbate the trouble, shall be avoided. (ii) Journalists and columnists owe a very special responsibility to their country in promoting communal peace and amity. Their writings are not a mere reflection of their own feelings but help to large extent in moulding the feelings and sentiments of the society at large. It is, therefore, of utmost importance that they use their pen with circumspection and restraint.[65]

---

[65] Clause 20, Norms of Journalistic Conduct, Press Council of India,

In light of this, the narrative-builders must not only introspect, but have to offer evidence to counter the mischief and falsity of these narratives. Tahir Hussain, a councillor of the Aam Aadmi Party (AAP), the ruling party in Delhi, has been arrested in connection with the Delhi riots and serious charges have been framed against him. Several videos have surfaced that show the terrace of his house on which petrol bombs (Molotov cocktails) were kept. Several dead bodies were recovered from a nullah/drain abutting his house. Tahir Hussain was arrested in connection with the murder of Ankit Sharma, a young Intelligence Bureau (IB) officer whose dead body was also found in the drain next to Hussain's house. At the time of writing this book, Tahir Hussain is in police custody and the police are trying to unearth a larger conspiracy. Another rioter, Shahrukh Pathan, who pointed a gun at a police officer, has also been arrested in Uttar Pradesh. When the video of Shahrukh Pathan brandishing the gun emerged, the narrative-builders could not succeed much in swaying the sentiments of the people because ample evidence to counter the narratives was available. Moreover, the Indian intelligence agencies were able to unearth a more sinister plot. There was a Pakistan angle to this story, which have been brought to the fore. The agencies also unearthed cross-country electronic chatter wherein people believed to be Pakistani operatives were berating their sources for not organizing enough crowds for anti-CAA protests on 3–4 March 2020, despite the funding at their

---

available at: http://presscouncil.nic.in/OldWebsite/NORMS-2010.pdf. Last accessed on 10 March 2020.

disposal.[66] The police have also discovered numerous social media accounts that were opened just before the start of the riots on 22 February 2020, and then closed on 26 February 2020, and how these accounts were used to instigate the riots, and provoke people.[67]

Shaheen Bagh Protests: Peaceful Protestors or Paid Provocateurs?

Shaheen Bagh is a Muslim-dominated locality in Delhi where several Muslim women were sitting in dissent against the CAA for over three months till the countrywide lockdown due to Covid-19 forced them to discontinue their public protest. This protest blocked the main arterial road and caused serious inconvenience to the people residing in the area. Several videos from the protests emerged in which individuals delivered speeches instigating Muslims against the incumbent government and against Hindus. Among the public, there was a growing resentment and anger against these protests which basically sought to hijack governance and control over public spaces. The narrative-builders have consistently tried to garner sympathy for the protestors. The organizers of the 'protest' have claimed that they have a fundamental right under Article 19(1)

---

[66] Shishir Gupta, 'Indian agencies point to Pak link in Anti CAA protests,' *Hindustan Times*, 7 March 2020, available at: https://www.hindustantimes.com/india-news/indian-agencies-point-to-pak-link-in-anti-caa-protests/story-qWCiqnXCO285Qsv1rFQJeL.html. Last accessed on 18 March 2020.

[67] 'Amit Shah on Delhi Violence: Social media used to incite hate, dozens of accounts closed', available at: https://www.indiatoday.in/india/story/delhi-violence-amit-shah-social-media-1654536-2020-03-11. Last accessed on 10 April 2020.

(a), which guarantees freedom of speech and expression, to carry out their sit-in protests and bring public life to a standstill. They forgot that there are several permissible restrictions that can be imposed on their freedom of speech in terms of Article 19(2). Moreover, the protests were causing inconvenience to the public at large.

The Supreme Court of India has made it clear that the right of the people at Shaheen Bagh to carry out protests did not supersede the rights of the general public. It made it clear that democracy works on expressing views, but there are lines and boundaries that control such expression and speech. The Court noted that blocking roads is a matter of grave concern. It is to be also noted that freedom of speech and expression does not extend to sympathizing with those accused of giving speeches instigating people to break India into pieces. The police arrested Sharjeel Imam, a former student of Jawaharlal Nehru University (JNU) for advocating the cutting off of Assam from India in a pamphlet that was distributed in mosques. In a speech he made at Jamia Millia Islamia and at Aligarh Muslim University (AMU), he suggested that 'India's chicken's neck, that is, the Assam–Bihar border, could be blocked to cut off the Centre and central forces' access to the Northeast states of India'.[68]

The video of the inflammatory speech at AMU by Sharjeel Imam, went viral. In the speech, Sharjeel Imam is heard saying, '*Assam aur India katke alag hojaaye, tabhi ye humari baat sunenge* (Only once India and Assam are cut off from

---

[68] Available at: https://www.indiatoday.in/india/story/sharjeel-imam-pamphlet-anti-caa-nrc-delhi-police-1642953-2020-02-03. Last accessed on 10 April 2020.

each other, will they listen to us)'. Protestors at Shaheen Bagh and elsewhere not only failed to condemn Sharjeel's speech but have in fact voiced their support for his call. During a Pride March of members of the LGBTQ+ community held at Azad Maidan in Mumbai, several slogans such as '*Sharjeel tere sapnoko hum manjil tak pahuchaenge* (Sharjeel, we will help realize your dreams)' were raised expressing solidarity with the cause which Sharjeel represents.[69] Subsequently, the sloganeers were booked under various provisions of the Indian Penal Code. As regards Shaheen Bagh, the protestors say they are not traitors.[70] However, in light of the several videos that have surfaced and in light of the sympathy and support expressed for the likes of Sharjeel, and also in light of the support to these protests from Pakistan,[71] one can see a nexus between a variety of actors and agencies that seek to destabilize India by instigating the Muslims to bring life to a standstill, provoke riots, and commit murder and mayhem.

---

[69] 'Slogans in support of Shaheen Bagh mastermind Sharjeel Imam, "Azaadi" and against CAA raised in Queer Mumbai Pride March 2020', *OpIndia*, 1 February 2020, available at: https://www.opindia.com/2020/02/sharjeel-imam-pro-azaadi-anti-caa-slogans-mumbai-queer-parade/. Last accessed on 10 March 2020.

[70] '"We love this country, stop calling us traitors", Shaheen Bagh protester tells mediators', *The Tribune*, 20 February 2020, available at: https://www.tribuneindia.com/news/we-love-this-country-stop-calling-us-traitors-shaheen-bagh-protester-tells-mediators-44565. Last accessed on 10 March 2020.

[71] 'Pakistan link to anti-CAA protests emerge, evidence of handlers reprimanding "sources" for failing to organise protest despite funds,' *OpIndia*, 7 March 2020, available at: https://www.opindia.com/2020/03/anti-caa-protests-pakistan-link-funds/. Last accessed on 10 March 2020.

Break Away from the Politics of Appeasement

By now it very much clear that the anti-CAA narrative is based on a political agenda of creating confusion and disruption. It is also clear that there is a growing resentment against the government after the abrogation of Article 370 and the Ram Mandir judgement. Over the decades since India gained Independence, Hindus never wore religion on their sleeve since they were taught by the narrative-builders to be apologetic about their own civilizational and cultural history. With the coming to power of the BJP-led government that had the stated agenda of nationalism and justice for all but appeasement of none, the majority community has begun to realize that their interest need not always be subservient to a minority veto. The current government has expressly rejected appeasement politics. In the past, Muslims were used as a political tool and appeasement politics was rampant. As an example, a reference may be made to the aftermath of the Shah Bano judgement.[72] In the Shah Bano case, the Supreme Court held that the right to claim maintenance under the relevant provision (Section 125) of the Code of Criminal Procedure is available to Muslim women as well. Subsequent to this judgement, which was a progressive step towards achieving gender justice for Muslim women, there were protests across the country. The then Congress government led by Rajiv Gandhi immediately bowed down and passed the Muslim Women (Protection of Rights on Divorce) Act, 1985, by virtue of which, the judgement of the Supreme Court was rendered ineffective and meaningless.

There have been numerous such instances of appeasement

---

[72] Mohd. Ahmed Khan vs Shah Bano Begum, AIR 1985 SC 945.

politics. In 2006, the then prime minister of India, Dr Manmohan Singh, went on record to state that Muslims should have the first right on state resources.[73] The present government, on the other hand, has made it clear that it will not resort to any appeasement politics, and as a vital step towards gender justice, for example, it has criminalized Triple Talaq, a practice which gave Muslim men the unilateral right to terminate marriage simply by pronouncing 'talaq' thrice. The Supreme Court had earlier condemned and struck down this practice as ultra vires of the Constitution of India.[74]

Historical Contexts

While debating the CAA, one would not be able to form an honest opinion without a good understanding of the entire matrix of historical events pertaining to the partitioning of India into an Islamic Republic of Pakistan and India, religious persecution of Hindus over centuries, various waves of migration, colonization and the British strategy of dividing and ruling, and how these issues have been addressed since the past 70 years. The Nehru–Liaquat Pact of 1950, for instance, which was signed by Jawaharlal Nehru and Liaquat Ali Khan on 8 April 1950 in Delhi, mandated that both India and Pakistan take care of their minorities. India has respected the mandate of the pact, but Pakistan has failed miserably in this regard. When India was partitioned in 1947, the share of Muslim population

---

[73] 'Muslims must have first claim on resources: PM', *The Times of India*, 9 December 2006, available at: http://timesofindia.indiatimes.com/articleshow/754937.cms?utm_source=contentofinterest&utm_medium=text&utm_campaign=cppst. Last accessed on 10 March 2020.
[74] Shayara Bano vs Union of India, (2017) 9 SCC 1.

in the country was 9.8 per cent—about three crore or 30 million in India. In 2019, the percentage of Muslim population in India is 14.2 per cent as per the 2011 Census, and that meant there are 17.22 crore or 172.2 million Muslims. The 2018 estimate of India's Muslim population was 201 million, making India the second-largest Muslim country in the world, after Indonesia. Whereas in Pakistan and Bangladesh, Hindu and Sikh population are almost on the verge of extinction and the statistics speak for themselves, and how the Nehru–Liaquat Pact was a great failure. The percentage of Hindus in West Pakistan at the time of Partition was about 15–20 per cent, and in East Pakistan, it was about 30 per cent. Now, in Pakistan (West Pakistan), Hindus are less than 1.6 per cent of the population and have been hounded day in, day out. In Bangladesh (erstwhile East Pakistan), the Hindu population is less than 9 per cent. Despite these stark figures, it is unbelievable that it is the Indian government and Hindus who are asked to mind their 'communal behaviour' whereas Muslims, as a general rule, and their enablers, both cry 'Islamophobia' and 'Hindu fundamentalism' when discussing Muslims and other minorities in the country.

The policies adopted by the then Congress government at the time of Partition created havoc in the life of the religious minorities in Pakistan, and they are now on the verge of extinction. The rest of the world, from the United Nations to local NGOs and the local 'secular' newspaper, instead, beat their breasts about 'Hindutva'. This level of blinkered, hateful and deceitful rhetoric ensures that India is almost always on the level of boil whenever there is a Hindu-majority government, meaning a BJP dispensation.

The persecuted religious minorities in 'Islamic Territory'

have no option other than to take shelter in India as their umbilical cord is attached to India.[75] It is necessary to take note of the correspondence between our leaders during the trying times of the post-Partition era. Sardar Patel wrote to Prime Minister Nehru on 2 September 1947, expressing his anguish at the fate of Hindus and Sikhs in Pakistan. He wrote: 'From morning till night these days, my time is here fully occupied with the talks of woe and atrocities which reach me through Hindu and Sikh refugees from all over Western Pakistan.'[76] Similarly, letters and telegrams by Prime Minister Nehru expressing his concerns about Hindus and Sikhs and the need to evacuate them from Sindh have been found. Regarding the policy of Pakistan towards the Sikh minorities, Leonard Mosley noted:

> Both (Indian and Pakistan) sides had signed, on 20 July, at Mountbatten's behest, a declaration that they would respect the rights of minorities. But Mountbatten was right in suspecting that they did not know what they were signing. The Sikh policy was to exterminate the Muslims in their midst. The Muslims, with their eyes on the rich Sikh farmlands, were content to drive the Sikhs out and only massacre those who insisted on remaining.[77]

---

[75] White Paper on Citizenship Amendment Act, Dr Syama Prasad Mookerjee Research Foundation, available at: https://www.spmrf.org/wp-content/uploads/2019/12/Citizenship-Amendment-Act.pdf. Last accessed on 13 March 2020.

[76] Durga Das (ed.), *Sardar Patel's Correspondence*, Vol. 4, Ahmadabad: Navajivan, 1972, p. 314.

[77] Leonard Mosely, *The Last Days of the British Raj*, Bombay: Jaico, 1960, p. 280.

In a speech made at a prayer meeting on 21 July 1947, Mahatma Gandhi had also expressed the thoughts that India would accept all Hindu refugees from Pakistan if they were to face oppression. An excerpt from that speech requires attention:

> The same friend from Pakistan then asks me: 'If all the Hindus of Pakistan or a very large number of them come away from Pakistan, will India give them shelter?' I think that such people should certainly be given shelter. However, if the well-to-do among them want to live in their old style, that will be difficult. In any case, they should certainly be given a place to live and they should be paid for their work. But I shall continue to hope that no non-Muslim will be forced to flee Pakistan out of fear and no Indian Muslim will flee his motherland.[78]

Unfortunately, the hope that Gandhiji expressed did not materialize and hundreds of thousands of non-Muslims were indeed forced to either convert or flee. Regarding the inclusion of displaced persons, Prime Minister Nehru had given an assurance in the Rajya Sabha on 5 November 1950:

> The Hon. Member referred to the question of citizenship. There is no doubt, of course, that those displaced persons who have come to settle in India are bound to have the citizenship. If the law is inadequate in this respect, the law should be changed.[79]

---

[78] White Paper on Citizenship Amendment Act, Dr Syama Prasad Mookerjee Research Foundation, p. 23, available at: https://www.spmrf.org/wp-content/uploads/2019/12/Citizenship-Amendment-Act.pdf. Last accessed on 13 March 2020.
[79] ibid.

Nehru had raised adequate concerns regarding the status of minorities in Pakistan:

> We also think of our brothers and sisters cut of us from by political boundaries and who unhappily cannot share present in the freedom that has come. They are of us and will remain of us whatever may happen, and we shall be sharers in their good and ill fortune alike.[80]

Dr Ambedkar, in his book, *Pakistan or the Partition of India*, had advocated for a complete exchange of population of Hindus and Muslims at the time of Partition. The following quote from his book is worth perusing:

> Some scoff at the idea of the shifting and exchange of population. But those who scoff can hardly be aware of the complications, which a minority problem gives rise to and the failures attendant upon almost all the efforts made to protect them. The constitutions of the post-war states, as well as of the older states in Europe which had a minority problem, proceeded on the assumption that constitutional safeguards for minorities should suffice for their protection and so the constitutions of most of the new states with majorities and minorities were studded with long lists of fundamental rights and safeguards to see that they were not violated by the majorities. What was the experience? Experience showed that safeguards did not save the minorities. Experience showed that even a ruthless war on the minorities did not solve the

---

[80] Pandit Jawaharlal Nehru during Declaration of Independence (Excerpt from 'Tryst with Destiny' speech on 14 August 1947, Parliament House).

problem. The states then agreed that the best way to solve it was for each to exchange its alien minorities within its border, for its own which was without its border, with a view to bring about homogeneous States. This is what happened in Turkey, Greece and Bulgaria. Those, who scoff at the idea of transfer of population, will do well to study the history of the minority problem, as it arose between Turkey, Greece and Bulgaria. If they do, they will find that these countries found that the only effective way of solving the minorities' problem lay in exchange of population. The task undertaken by the three countries was by no means a minor operation. It involved the transfer of some 20 million people from one habitat to another. But undaunted, the three shouldered the task and carried it to a successful end because they felt that the considerations of communal peace must outweigh every other consideration. That the transfer of minorities is the only lasting remedy for communal peace is beyond doubt. If that is so, there is no reason why the Hindus and the Muslims should keep on trading in safeguards which have proved so unsafe. If small countries, with limited resources like Greece, Turkey and Bulgaria, were capable of such an undertaking, there is no reason to suppose that what they did cannot be accomplished by Indians. After all, the population involved is inconsiderable and because some obstacles require to be removed, it would be the height of folly to give up so sure a way to communal peace.[81]

---

[81] Dr B.R. Ambedkar, Pakistan or the Partition of India, extract available at: http://www.sacw.net/article2880.html. Last accessed on 13 March 2020.

India saw several waves of migration from both East Pakistan and West Pakistan, a significant wave being the one in 1950, when there were rampant attacks on non-Muslims. Pakistan had institutionalized hate against its religious minorities. Liaquat Ali Khan, in his address to the nation on Pakistan's third Independence Day, stated ominously and in a celebratory fashion:

> Let us so live and act that hundreds of years hence when history recalls our times it will say: These people lived, struggled and suffered like true sons of Islam so that their children may live in honour and glory.[82]

In this context, we can even look at some extracts from the report, 'Recurrent Exodus of Minorities from East Pakistan and Disturbances in India, 1965':

> After 1950 killings with which we shall presently deal, the Hindu holdings of properties fell to 12.7% and nearly 90% of Hindu citizen of Dacca migrated to India. Similar is the case with the student population in Dacca. From 2,900 Hindu boys in schools before Partition, 2,000 remained before February 1950 killings. And at the end of December 1950 the number was reduced to 140. Similarly, there were about 2,100 Hindu girls in schools before Partition, about 1,200 before the February 1950 incident. Of these only 25 remained by December 1950. The population of Hindu college students fell from 65% at Partition to 7% in January 1950 and at the end of 1950

---

[82] Liaquat Ali Khan's address to the nation on Pakistan's Independence Day, 14 August 1950.

only 12 remained. Similar is the case with lawyers. There were about 1,500 Hindu shops at the time of Partition and at the end of 1950 only 157 remained. In each of the 45 big and small towns, with the exception of the five smaller ones, Hindu inhabitants were in majority though taking the total population the number of Hindus amounted to 30%.[83]

The data on the year-wise influx of non-Muslim migrants from Bangladesh is available in the Lok Sabha records as of 1959, which also makes for distressing reading[84]:

Period	Influx (in lakh/100,000 persons)
Up to December 1949	13.78
During 1950	15.82
During 1951 & 1952	3.92
During 1953	0.76
During 1954	1.18
During 1955	2.39
During 1956	3.20
During 1957	0.11
During 1958 (up to 31 March 1958)	0.01
Total	**41.17**

---

[83] Extracts from 'Recurrent Exodus of Minorities from East Pakistan and Disturbances in India, 1965', p. 4. Available at: https://www.icj.org/wp-content/uploads/2013/06/India-minorities-East-Pakistan-fact-finding-report-1965-eng.pdf.
[84] Estimate supplied to Lok Sabha, 1959.

There was another wave of migration in 1964. In March 1958, certain restrictions were imposed on migration from East Pakistan. But even then, the migration continued. In 1962, there were organized riots and assaults on the minority communities in Rajshahi and other adjacent districts of East Pakistan and about 20,000-25,000 people migrated to India. Then came the riots in January-February of 1964. This time the riots were more well-planned and widespread than even the riots of 1950. The number of casualties is anybody's guess, but it ran into the tens of thousands. The rate of influx of migrants from January 1964 onwards assumed serious proportions, and this time even Buddhists and Christians were also harassed. It led to another mass migration from East Pakistan into India. A large number of the tribal population also migrated both after the Rajshahi riots of 1962 and after the last riots of 1964. Distressing reports were received of harassment of migrants including assaults on women, robbery and physical violence on a large scale in the course of the migrants' journey across the border.[85] The data available with the Lok Sabha in 1964 indicates that about 8,56,000 people entered West Bengal, Assam and Tripura from East Pakistan. As per a statement given in Parliament by the Minister of State for External Affairs on 13 August 1970, only 6,21,805 Hindus remained in West Pakistan while there were 93,79,669 Hindus in East Pakistan.[86] A large number of refugees from East Pakistan moved to India during 1971. Commenting on the status of such refugees in India, Prime Minister Indira Gandhi said:

---

[85] Ministry of Rehabilitation, Estimates Committee, 1964-65, Third Lok Sabha.
[86] Official number given by Surendra Pal Singh, Minister of State, Ministry of External Affairs in Rajya Sabha on 13 August 1970 (Census of 1961).

> So massive a migration, in so short a time, is unprecedented in recorded history. About three and a half million people have come into India from Bangladesh during the last eight weeks... They come from every social class and age group. They are not refugees in the sense we have understood this word since Partition. They are victims of war who have sought refuge from the military terror across our frontier.[87]

Do we hear any of this in the context of the present-day orchestrated campaigns by Muslims and their enablers? No, not one little bit because it will not fit into their narrative of victimhood and 'Hindu fascism' and 'Hindu nationalism'.

Hypocrisy of Those Opposing the CAA

It is clear that once it became evident that the CAA would soon be passed by Parliament, several Opposition leaders from parties such as the Congress party, Trinamool Congress (TMC), Communist Party of India (Marxist) [CPI (M)], Janata Dal (Secular), and others have come down heavily on the government. They have called the CAA exclusionist. Some have stated that the Act is ultra vires the Constitution, as it compromises on the secular credentials of India. However, it is clear that the vehement opposition to the CAA today is out of sheer political expediency and of animosity. Even the communist leaders have, in the past, taken up the issue of religious persecution in East Pakistan. For example, Bhupesh Gupta, Member of Parliament (CPI), made an extensive speech

---

[87] Prime Minister Indira Gandhi, Lok Sabha, 24 May 1971.

in the Rajya Sabha, on 4 March 1964, and here is an excerpt:

> It seems, Sir, since we signed the Nehru-Liaquat Pact, we went into some kind of sleep, became a little complacent, perhaps because there were no major riots. But it was a mistake. We should have always taken up the cause of the minorities. Sir, especially when the agreement, which has some kind of international force, the Nehru-Liaquat Pact, was being violated by Pakistan, it was our duty to have informed the world public opinion through the diplomatic levels and also otherwise. I regret to say that we did not do so. Maybe we had been mistaken out of good intentions or some miscalculations, being on the good side of things. But life has shown that we have been complacent in this matter and we should have functioned a little differently in this matter.[88]

In a resolution adopted by the CPI(M) in 2012 at Kozhikode during its 20th Congress, the CPI(M) had taken an emphatic stand on the issue of Bangladeshi minorities and had in fact demanded an amendment to Section 2(1)(b) of the Citizenship Act, the very provision that now stands amended. The relevant extract from that resolution reads as follows:

> This Party Congress demands a suitable amendment in Clause 2 (i) (b) of the said Citizenship Act in relation to the Bangladesh minority community refugees. This must be done while protecting the Assam accord which is

---

[88] White Paper on Citizenship Amendment Act, Dr Syama Prasad Mookerjee Research Foundation, p. 28, available at: https://www.spmrf.org/wp-content/uploads/2019/12/Citizenship-Amendment-Act.pdf. Last accessed on 13 March 2020.

relevant to the specific situation in Assam. It demands that the Central Government bring such an amendment in the forthcoming budget session of Parliament. It assures these communities the support of the CPI (M) in their struggle for their genuine demands.[89]

There are several other relevant statements of the Communist Party's leaders both on the floor of the House and outside Parliament, in speeches and resolutions. All such statements need not be reproduced here, but we need to point out the hypocrisy of the communists and the political nature of this entire debate.

In 2012, Tarun Gogoi, the then chief minister of Assam and a leader of the Congress party, had submitted a memorandum to the then prime minister, Dr Manmohan Singh, pleading that Indian citizens who had to flee due to discrimination and religious persecution at the time of Partition, should not be treated as foreigners.[90] In fact, Gogoi had, on several occasions, taken up the issue of Hindu refugees from Bangladesh. In 2014, he had urged Prime Minister Modi to bring about a policy on giving asylum to Hindu refugees from Bangladesh. In 2011 as well, he went on record to state that Bengali Hindus were a persecuted lot in Bangladesh.[91] The

---

[89] White Paper on Citizenship Amendment Act, Dr Syama Prasad Mookerjee Research Foundation, p. 35, available at: https://www.spmrf.org/wp-content/uploads/2019/12/Citizenship-Amendment-Act.pdf. Last accessed on 13 March 2020.

[90] ibid. p.27.

[87] 'Concept of Religious Persecution – How Congress Ridiculing the Idea That Itself Proposed in the Past', *The True Picture*, 23 December 2019, available at: https://www.thetruepicture.org/tarun-gogoi-bangladeshi-hindus-religious-persecution-caa/. Last accessed on 13 March 2020.

Assam Pradesh Congress Committee had, in 2015, declared:

> We will take up the unsolved issue of Citizenship for Bengali Hindus, Buddhists and Christians and people of other minority communities who came to Assam after being subjected to inhuman torture post the partition of India.[92]

In 2003, Dr Manmohan Singh, in the capacity of Leader of the Opposition in the Rajya Sabha, had also said:

> After the partition of our country, minorities in countries like Bangladesh have faced persecution, and it is our moral obligation that if circumstances force people, these unfortunate people, to seek refuge in our country, our approach to granting citizenship to these unfortunate persons should be more liberal.[93]

The statement of former minister of external affairs, Pranab Mukherjee, is also to be noted. While speaking in the Rajya Sabha, he stated:

> Reports of violence and atrocities against minorities including Hindus in Bangladesh are received from time to time. It has been conveyed at the highest levels of government that such incidents have an adverse impact on public sentiment in India, which in turn have potential of affecting bilateral ties, and should be strictly dealt with.[94]

---

[92] Assam Pradesh Congress Committee (APCC) on 1 June 2015.
[93] Dr Manmohan Singh's speech in the Rajya Sabha, 18 December 2003.
[94] Pranab Mukherjee's speech in the Rajya Sabha, 6 December 2007.

Prakash Karat, the general secretary of the CPI(M), had written a letter in 2012 to Dr Manmohan Singh, who was then prime minister. The letter asked for bringing changes in the citizenship procedure which are similar to those included in the CAA. Here is an extract from the letter:

> This is to draw your attention to the citizenship problems of a large number of refugees from erstwhile East Bengal and then even after formation of Bangladesh who had to flee their country in particular historical circumstances over which they had no control. Their situation is different from those who come to India due to economic reasons. While we advocate humane approach to all sections, on the specific issue of citizenship we share the opinion you had strongly advocated as leader of the opposition when it was debated in Parliament in 2003.[95]

The Hindu Bengali refugees, many of whom are from the socially disempowered Dalit community, are victims of circumstances and have been exploited by successive regimes but have never got their due. For example, the Matua community from Bengal, which originally backed the CPI(M) but later shifted to the TMC, after the former prioritized help of Muslims over their support and the latter promised to take care of their concerns. One of them was their long-pending demand to be granted Indian citizenship. The TMC gained a lot of votes in the 2009 general elections and the 2011 assembly elections, on the support of the Matua community. However, the TMC did not bring the concerns of the Matua community to the

---

[95] Letter written by Mr Prakash Karat, General Secretary (CPIM) to Dr Manmohan Singh, the then prime minister, dated 3 June 2012.

UPA, of which the TMC was a part of till 2013. Now, when the CAA, initiated by the BJP, has paved the way for the Matua community to realize their dream, it is Mamata Banerjee's party that is doing everything to scuttle it. On the one hand, she opposed the NRC in Assam and said she could not support it because that would compel Bengalis to leave India. On the other hand, Mamata Banerjee's party ensured that the CAB did not sail through the Rajya Sabha, even after the BJP made it clear that it would protect the interests of persecuted Hindu Bengali refugees. It is quite clear that her opposition to the NRC or her concerns about the CAB is not dictated by genuine concern for the Hindu Bengali refugees but cynical vote bank politics. She only seems to care for the illegal Bangladeshi Muslim migrants, who she thinks, can assure her victory in future elections.[96]

Another prominent political figure who had called for protection of the interests of the persecuted religious minorities is Ashok Gehlot of the Congress party, who is also the incumbent chief minister of Rajasthan. On 6 March 2002, in his capacity as chief minister, he had written a letter to L.K. Advani, then home minister, bringing to his attention, the plight of the minority communities from Pakistan who had settled in Rajasthan. He had called upon Advani to take steps to give powers to the district collectors and additional collectors in Rajasthan to grant citizenship to members of these persecuted minorities.[97] In September 2004, he again wrote

---

[96] White Paper on Citizenship Amendment Act, Dr Syama Prasad Mookerjee Research Foundation, p. 21, available at: https://www.spmrf.org/wp-content/uploads/2019/12/Citizenship-Amendment-Act.pdf. Last accessed on 13 March 2020.

[97] Letter dated 6 March 2002 by Ashok Gehlot, Hon'ble Chief Minister,

to Shivraj Patil, then home minister in the UPA government, requesting him to take steps in this regard. The letter specifically makes a mention of 'Hindu refugees' from Pakistan.[98] In fact, the National Democratic Alliance (NDA) government, led by Prime Minister Atal Bihari Vajpayee, on 28 February 2004, had brought an amendment to the Citizenship Rules, 1956, to facilitate citizenship for persecuted Hindus from Pakistan, and for those refugees to be settled in four districts of Gujarat and two districts in Rajasthan. This rule was subsequently extended by the Congress party-led UPA government for a period of one year through a notification dated 22 February 2005, and then again for another year vide notification dated 12 July 2006. The rule remained in force for three years till 2007, well within the UPA's tenure.

Abul Barkat, a professor of economics at Dhaka University, notes that around 113 lakh (11.3 million) Hindus left Bangladesh between the years 1964 and 2013 due to religious persecution. He expresses the fear that by 2050 there will be no Hindu left in Bangladesh.[99] His apprehension has been ignored by the vested interests who have combined to corner the BJP on this matter of granting citizenship under the CAA.

Rajasthan, to L.K. Advani, Hon'ble Home Minister, Government of India.
[98] Letter dated 15 September 2004 by Ashok Gehlot, General Secretary, All India Congress Committee, to Shivraj Patil, Hon'ble Home Minister, Government of India.
[99] Md. Kamrul Hasan, 'No Hindus will be left after 30 years', *Dhaka Tribune*, 20 November 2016, available at: https://www.dhakatribune.com/bangladesh/2016/11/20/abul-barkat-632-hindus-left-country-day/. Last accessed on 14 April 2020.

Concluding Note

It is thus clear that the entire debate on the CAA, and the violent protests and the riots that have been engineered are all part of a political scheme aimed at unsettling the BJP government and creating an atmosphere of fear and anxiety in the country. This is not just any old opposition tactics or hypocrisy but political gamesmanship that threatens the very foundations of a democratic India. The strategy of the Opposition and the narrative-builders is to create confusion and chaos in the mind of the common man. The Opposition parties, in this endeavour, have left no stone unturned, and the vested interests in the media, higher education institutions and activist NGOs, with some dangerous and deep connections to actors and activists outside India, have all contributed to these attempts to derail the present government. Their narrative, spun together by sophisticated and glib wordsmiths, whose ideological blinkers blind them to reality, is not enough to shake this government for the simple reason that their narrative not only is shorn of facts or logic, and is legally unsound, but the majority of Indians reject their attempt to divide India and undermine the great Indian civilizational ethos. The CAA is not against the spirit of the Constitution of India but is, in fact, the nurturing spirit that will strengthen the spirit of the Indian ethos.

A CASE OF MISDIRECTION

SALMAN KHURSHID

To Mahira Sayyed: Freedom's Child

Author's Note

The CAA debate was loud and intense with allusions of patriotism used vigorously by both sides. Since the TV channels dominated the debate, and being self-opinionated, they seldom feel obliged to treat a debate on important public issues as two or more legitimate points of view, the opportunity that Rupa Publications provided to explore the two competing viewpoints came as a great opportunity to strengthen democracy. I took up the challenge in right earnest even as the format proposed was somewhat novel. Although the format of author versus author has to be adhered to as a matter of aesthetics and integrity, I owe it to my colleague, Aadya Mishra, who has made this work possible with her tireless research and some sound formulations. She has the makings of a fine lawyer and prepared a compelling brief for constitutional dimensions of the debate.

The sudden, though some people might say not so sudden, onset of the COVID-19 pandemic guillotined the CAA debate and the related protests. In times of such deep crisis and challenge to the human race, one would expect political and ideological fault lines to be diluted, if not, entirely obliterated. Yet, the belligerent self-righteousness that we saw in the CAA arguments has permeated the public scrutiny of our collective response to the virus. Even as we look for a preventive vaccine and a cure for COVID-19, we have to learn to talk to each other, political parties, social organizations, communities and ordinary people. Hopefully, this book will help us all take a step in that direction.

Situating Citizenship

Citizenship, conceptually and practically, has a close proximity to the territorial identity and collective sovereignty of people of a particular country (described sometimes in conjunction with domicile). It denotes a sense of belonging to the country one lives in, a feeling of patriotism. It is a concept with roots in the ancient Greek civilization where it had a pivotal role in the affairs of the nation state. As time passed, the structure of society became complex and travel grew: citizenship attributes and the concept of travel permits and passports became familiar to everyday existence. The Second World War brought in a stricter, more complex situation for countries at war and in post-war situation.

Citizenship also came to be relevant for people who are not original residents of a territory but persecuted individuals who sought safety from oppression by their own national governments. Persecuted German Jews, the survivors of the holocaust, became displaced, languishing in 'displaced persons camps' for years. Unwilling to resettle in their home country and faced with excessive restrictions placed by other Western nations, the British Mandate for Palestine became their refuge. Local Arabs' opposition to Jewish emigration and continuing stringent laws in neighbouring countries of the Soviet Bloc prolonged their anxiety till Israel gained Independence in 1948, bringing into effect the termination of the British Mandate. Since then, the problem has acquired another dimension with some Arabs being citizens of the Jewish State of Israel and others losing out to Israeli settlements. In the Indian context, the Partition of 1947 caused a wave of legislation that distinguished between citizens and non-citizens. The earliest post-Partition legislation was the evacuee property legislation which, in essence, allowed the State to acquire title of vacated lands of emigrating Muslim population of India and resettling the Hindu and Sikh refugees from the newly created West and East Pakistan.

Interestingly, in the Indian legal landscape, nationality and citizenship are linguistically treated as interchangeable. This is quite different from countries like the Central Asian republics, such as Uzbekistan and Kazakhstan. A person can be of German descent and therefore claim German nationality and yet be a citizen of Uzbekistan or Kazakhstan as the case might be. There would be other citizens who are ethnically of Uzbek or Kazakh descent. Many Uzbeks, Kazakhs and Turks (from Turkistan) are important citizens of Afghanistan where Pashtun, Hazara and Afghans are their compatriots. In the West, there are Blacks (once called 'coloured' or 'Negroes') who are now referred to as Afro-Americans just as Indian and Pakistani migrants are referred to as South Asians. Many countries in the West permit dual citizenship as is the case with the US and Israeli citizenship and the UK. Countries across the world are getting used to multi-ethnic citizenship that includes people of various origins. Whilst conservative ideologies attempt to ring fence migration by actions like US President Donald Trump building a border wall to keep Mexicans out of the US, the reality of second-generation migrant children dominating public space, even holding top positions in public life, academics, industry and sports, is also fast emerging. Going by their profiles and success stories, the world becoming a global village no longer seems like a distant dream. We Indians proudly applaud the success and influence of our diaspora.

Apart from the regular immigration policies that have certainly been of mutual benefit to the migrants as well as their adopted countries, there have also been periodic surges of refugees escaping from natural or man-made disasters, the most recent one being the unrest in the Arab world and large-scale movement of refugees to Europe. It is here that we need to take note of the international effort to provide succour and support to refugees, as indeed, endorse the global effort to eliminate statelessness or reduce it to a minimum. Sadly, despite our excellent humanitarian credentials, we have yet to adopt a clear policy on refugees that would naturally accommodate the currently targeted category.

Post-Partition of 1947, after a few months of unregulated movement across the new borders, the Emergency Permit System of 1948 was introduced in quick succession by Pakistan and India to regulate the large influx of Hindu and Muslim populations from their respective sides of the border, subjecting people to increasing surveillance and scrutiny, supplementing and not exclusive of the Evacuee Property legislation in the two countries. It was intended to impose restrictions on the movement of refugees primarily focused on the western border. The Constitution of India adopted in 1950 provides for citizenship of the country as follows:

(a) Article 5 of the Constitution granted citizenship at the commencement of the Constitution to every person who

has his domicile in the territory of India and being born in the territory of India; or
(b) either of whose parents was born in the territory of India; or
(c) who has been ordinarily resident in the territory of India for not less than five years immediately preceding such commencement.

Vide Article 6, notwithstanding anything in Article 5, a person who migrated to India from Pakistan before 19 July 1948 and ordinarily resident of the country whose parents or any of the grandparents were born in India could claim citizenship. Any such person coming after the cut-off date was required to register having been in the territory for six months. The latter category included persons who had migrated to Pakistan but returned to India under permit for resettlement or permanent return. Such persons living abroad too could claim citizenship by registering with the Indian mission there.

In 1955, the Citizenship Act expanded the categories and provided citizenship by birth to persons born in India after 26 January 1950 but before 1 July 1987; or after that cut-off but before commencement of the Amendment Act, 2003, provided either of the parents is an Indian citizen; however for those born after 2003, both parents were required to be Indian citizens, or at least one of them, and the other not an illegal migrant.

The Citizenship Act, 1955, brought in a distinction between citizens and non-citizens by defining 'illegal migrants' under Section 2(b) of the said Act. The Permit System introduced by the governments of Pakistan and India to regulate movement of individuals in the months after Partition was subsequently replaced with the Passport System in 1967 by an Act of Parliament in India. (Pakistan's Passport Act came into force in 1974.) All the legislations so made were in consonance with Part II and III of the Constitution of India. The Supreme Court of India, however, pursued a policy of narrow interpretation with respect to the legal question of granting citizenship to alleged migrants in several judgements that followed (discussed later).

The Citizenship Act, over the years, has been subject to several amendments addressing legal-political issues relevant to those times. However the most recent amendment to the Act in 2019 (CAA) has become the most controversial piece of legislation with huge swathes of people coming together spontaneously across the country and worldwide to oppose its implementation. The aforementioned concept of 'illegal migrants' finds its relevance dramatically modified by this new amendment with the exclusion of persons belonging to six religions, namely, Hindus, Jains, Buddhists, Sikhs, Parsis and Christians from a select few countries—Pakistan, Bangladesh and Afghanistan—on grounds of their persecution in their home countries. This has generated apprehension in the minds of Muslims in India that in conjunction with the NPR, and NRC, those excluded from the benefit of the amendment will eventually become unwanted stateless persons. Furthermore, Dalits and generally poor persons of all religions have a special concern that they might not be able to match the standards of proof under the NRC and equally come to grief. But besides concern about their personal prospects, a growing number are asserting their right to uphold the Constitution and constitutional governance, and that of the excluded minorities from other neighbouring countries such as Sri Lanka, Myanmar and Bhutan.

Even as people took to protest marches and massive sit-ins to show defiance of the CAA, NRC and NPR, the government was adamant in its response and sought to defend its position partly on manufactured logic and partly on the supposed history of endorsement by none other than Mahatma Gandhi himself, and not to mention contradictory statements on the decision to implement the NRC.

The BJP government, with a penchant for pulling rabbits out of their political hat, let loose cheerleaders to sing paeans and media spin doctors got to work not so much to persuade naysayers and cynics but aggressively to ridicule doubters as anti-nationals in connivance with Left-wing student leaders like Kanhaiya Kumar and the so-called Lutyens' elite and Khan Market gang.[100] This time, additionally in a heroic effort made to marshal advocates for CAA, the governor of Kerala, Arif Mohammad Khan, all too eager to join the battle, was pressed into service. But what must be taken seriously is the categorical support of Harish Salve, a distinguished leader of the Bar and former law officer of the Indian government.

It would be interesting, if not edifying, to know whether Governor Khan learnt his history from Amit Shah or vice versa. In any case, they both profess to be deeply committed to what they believe Gandhi and Nehru said about 'opening our hearts and doors to Hindus and Sikhs from Pakistan'. It would, of course, have been wonderful if they followed the two great leaders in other matters like compassion and secularism. Be that as it may, it is far from clear if this is an ideological position or strategic political choice.

---

[100] A reference to the supposed meeting point for people opposed to the sitting government.

In recent weeks, we have been repeatedly told that it was Gandhi's wish and Nehru's commitment that migrant Hindus and Sikhs be provided citizenship and jobs. To put the record straight, the Partition assumed that people could choose to stay put or migrate across the newly drawn borders. But obviously many Muslims, though certainly far from all, were expected to cross over to Pakistan just as most Hindus were expected to cross over to India. *The Long Partition and the Making of South Asia* by Vazira Fazila-Yacoobali Zamindar[101] tells us that in Sindh, the steady departure of Hindus was seen as sad even as the stream of Muslims coming from India was thought to be unwanted. The grand vision of a Muslim homeland floundered on the waves of Muhajirs (Muslim refugees) entering Pakistan. Ultimately, the crossings at Kokrapar were closed because more migrants could not be accommodated. In India, there was an issue of dealing with Muslims who returned after having initially migrated to Pakistan (95,000 registered after the Nehru–Liaquat Pact) as well as Hindus and Sikhs who took belated decision to leave Pakistan despite Jinnah's assurances. Arif Khan makes that as the mainstay of his argument as indeed adding allegations of some unspeakable atrocities of sexual exploitation that should have been brought to the notice of the United Nations Human Rights Council. Initially, people crossed the border without papers, then travel permits were introduced and finally, the India–Pakistan passports were issued by the two sides. At that point, the documents authorized travel but were not yet associated with citizenship.

---

[101] Vazira Fazila-Yacoobali Zamindar. *The Long Partition and the Making of Modern South Asia: Refugees, Boundaries, Histories.* Columbia University Press, 2010.

Mahatma Gandhi's response to Hindu and Sikh immigrants must be understood in the context that most of them had already migrated to India at the time of Partition under the exchange of population approach in Punjab. Even so, Gandhi's statement is cleverly and selectively used to support the negation of his message. In his statement beyond the part quoted, Gandhi had gone on to welcome Muslims as well. We must not forget that Gandhi was preparing to travel to Pakistan when he was treacherously assassinated.

The problem posed by returning Muslims was that their properties had been vested to the custodian of evacuee property and in many cases, utilized for settling refugees. There was no issue about their citizenship really and, therefore, it did not figure in conversations. On the other hand, there are examples like letters written to migrants in Pakistan by Dr Zakir Husain, the former president of India, pleading with them to return home. I know of individuals who returned after some months and even wrote about one such case in my book, *At Home in India*.[102] It is quite understandable that Hindus and Sikhs who might otherwise have migrated at the time of Partition chose to do so as a second thought, disappointed with conditions in Pakistan. But that applies just as much to Muslims from Pakistan, as we know, several hundred have been granted citizenship of India over the years. The problem with the CAA is that it seeks to create an artificial divide between Hindus and Sikhs on the one hand and Muslims on the other, seemingly on grounds of persecution, although the law, as passed, does not require any proof of persecution. The truth is that many

---

[102] Salman Khurshid, *At Home in India: The Muslim Saga*. Hay House India, 2014.

Muslims, particularly Qadiani, Shias and those belonging to Baloch tribes, face much worse persecution. We could simply have made a law to accommodate refugees keeping the historical and regional context in mind, or indeed, used the existing law with the mentioned context in mind, without violating constitutional norms. Furthermore, by accepting Muslims who reject Pakistan, we would underscore our consistent rejection of the two-nation theory.

Arif Khan also suggested that since Partition, there has been a severe drop in Pakistan's non-Muslim population although he might be exaggerating by collapsing the figures of Pakistan and Bangladesh. That still does not justify automatic exclusion of migrant or refugee Muslims from our concern. His reference to the All India Congress Committee (AICC) Resolution[103] and concern expressed by Ashok Gehlot, the then chief minister of Rajasthan, must remain in the context of a pending issue that any reasonable person would want resolved. It certainly cannot add any ideological dimension to justify the thesis Arif Khan proposes. We must not forget that despite Khan's exertion, we are not limited to the India–Pakistan binary but are dealing with Bangladesh and Afghanistan as well. The logic applied to Pakistan's treatment of its minority might not serve

---

[103] The AICC Working Committee resolution of 27 September read '...The Congress is further bound to afford full protection to all those non-Muslims from Pakistan who have crossed the border and come over to India or may do so to save their life and honour. It expects of these entrants to accept loyally the democratic and non-communal basis of the Constitution...' Available at: https://www.indiatoday.in/india/story/arif-mohammad-khan-pinarayi-vijayan-anti-caa-para-kerala-governor-assembly-speech-watch-video-1641130-2020-01-29. Last accessed on 10 April 2020.

Bangladesh and certainly not Afghanistan about which former president, Hamid Karzai, has said all its citizens are persecuted because of civil war. Furthermore, excluding Sri Lanka defies logic.

Having lent CAA moral agnosticism, Arif Khan has opted to steer clear of the response in Assam where people and the government have uniformly opposed the law because their concern is about outsiders who will dilute their culture, irrespective of their faith. It is this that leads one to believe that the persecution story is a ruse for resolving the problem of what to do with the Hindu foreigners identified in the NRC process in Assam. Beyond that, there is doubt that the same preferential treatment will be extended to people of particular faith under the proposed nationwide NRC to be conducted. In view of that, the apprehension expressed by people across the country cannot be swept aside with snide comments about devious intentions.

The repeated performances by the governor in his own state, and in appearances from New Delhi to Varanasi, not to mention several media salvos, underscore two points about public discourse: first, if a falsehood is repeated several times, it becomes the truth; and second, preaching to the converted makes the art of distortion of truth somewhat easy. But it takes a brave man to teach history to Professor Irfan Habib as the governor sought to do at the Indian History Congress.[104]

Whatever scholarship doubts one might have about the governor will not stand up to a top lawyer of our country who had generously accepted, pro bono, briefs on behalf of the

---

[104] C.P. Sajit, 'Indian History Congress did not invite Governor: Irfan Habib,' *The Hindu*, 29 December 2019.

government to wrest the Nizam's bank deposits from Pakistan (under the UPA) and secure the life of Kulbhushan Jadav at the International Court of Justice (under the NDA). Harish Salve's defence of the CAA must indeed be considered carefully.

Salve says that the principle of equality would not result in taking away from the State the power of making classification. If a law deals equally with members of a defined class, it is not open to the charge of denial of equal protection on the ground, he argues, that it has no application to other persons citing the CAA's avowed objective to enable conferment of Indian citizenship upon members of minority communities who hail from Afghanistan, Bangladesh and Pakistan. It is a law that is designed to confer the benefit on an identified class of persons, and that identification is based on a rational criterion.[105] But that begs the question.

Furthermore, all this seems somewhat reductionist. Of course the government can choose a class or category to give the benefit of citizenship, but how does one accept that a rational criterion has been applied? Is merely stating that there is a rationale behind it enough? Or is a disclosure of rational grounds called for? Can, as Arif Khan suggests, it be enough to cite the wishes of Nehru and Gandhi that we, of course, would honour or would the legal test of reasonable classification still have to be satisfied? It is no argument that Salve makes, that including all communities from the neighbouring countries will obliterate the borders. We will need to know why religious

---

[105] Harish Salve, 'CAA is necessary: Why the many arguments about its being unconstitutional don't hold water', *The Times of India*, 5 March 2020, available at: https://timesofindia.indiatimes.com/blogs/toi-edit-page/caa-is-necessary-why-the-many-arguments-about-its-being-unconstitutional-dont-hold-water/. Last accessed on 3 April 2020.

persecution alone meets the test and not persecution per se.

Salve goes on to say, 'The Prime Minister has denied it. If any procedure put in place requires Muslims alone all over India to prove their citizenship in a manner more onerous than that applicable to any other community, such a procedure would be unconstitutional.'[106] It may well be that such an intent cannot be expressly established but to use a phrase of Justice D.Y. Chandrachud, the consequences might have a 'chilling effect'. Salve, of all people, surely knows the 'pith and substance test'.[107]

Do we really need proof that religious minorities are persecuted in these Islamic republics? That is an interesting question and in today's India, it would be politically incorrect to remotely doubt it. But we live in an interdependent diplomatic world and unless we have decided to sour our relations with three important neighbours, we surely cannot publicly accuse them of vile persecution of their minorities and get back to business as usual.

Salve justifies the classification excluding Muslims by underscoring the special provisions made for minorities in the Constitution. But that amounts to saying that reverse discrimination or affirmative action justifies discrimination in the first place once the category is established.

Fortunately, several former judges have voiced their opinion that fortifies the contrary view and negates any attempt to describe it as politically motivated. Former chief justice of Delhi High Court, A.P. Shah, has said that there could

---

[106] Available at: https://www.newindianexpress.com/nation/2020/mar/05/caa-is-necessary-not-meant-to-send-muslims-out-of-india-says-top-lawyer-harish-salve-2112705.html. Last accessed on 23 March 2020.
[107] Synthetics and Chemicals vs UP (1990) 1 SCC 109.

be no second opinion about the fact that the CAA violates the Constitution. He said it negates the guarantee of Article 14 on equal treatment under the law, at five different levels. It was neither reasonable nor rational but, in fact, arbitrary. Furthermore, it was difficult to understand the deadline of 31 December 2014. It suggested that either persecution of minorities stopped after that date, or the Indian government did not care about it. Similarly, Abhinav Chandrachud, advocate and author, made a brilliant analysis in a lecture in Mumbai, clearly showing the CAA to be in violation of Article 14.[108]

With growing scepticism internationally[109] and continuing adverse reportage in the international media, it was inevitable that the minister of external affairs and a brilliant former diplomat, S. Jaishankar, should take up cudgels for a bad cause. When asked about the CAA at the ET Global Business Summit, Jaishankar said, 'We have tried to reduce the number of stateless people through this legislation. That should be appreciated.'[110] But that begs the question. Migrants from Pakistan or elsewhere are not stateless persons; they are merely hoping to give up their citizenship and become Indian citizens. On the other hand, there is now a real danger that people who have always believed they are Indian citizens and have no other connections will suddenly be told that they are stateless

---

[108] Abhinav Chandrachud at Mumbai Collective, Brut on Facebook, available at: https://www.facebook.com/brutindia/videos/153109652384364/. Last accessed on 15 April 2020.

[109] See comments by Supreme Leader of Iran and President of Turkey as well as legislators from the UK and the US.

[110] Available at: https://economictimes.indiatimes.com/news/politics-and-nation/unhrc-skirting-around-cross-border-terror-issue-in-jk-jaishankar-at-et-gbs-2020/articleshow/74543859.cms?from=mdr. Last accessed on 23 March 2020.

persons. The Minister further argued, '[E]very body, when they look at citizenship, have a context and has a criterion. Show me a country in the world which says everybody in the world is welcome. Nobody says that.'[111] But the issue is not about who is welcome; rather it is about who is not, and why. Asked if India was losing its friends, the Minister responded: 'Maybe we are getting to know who our friends really are.'[112] When world leaders warn India of threat of isolation, it may be myopic to console ourselves with the discovery of truth.

Being Economical with the Truth: What the CAA, NRC and NPR Mean Together

The CAA has raised an unprecedented furore in the country. The amendment to the Act redefines 'illegal migrants' under Section 2(1)(b) of the principal Act of 1955 by exempting specifically six minority religious communities, namely, Hindus, Sikhs, Buddhists, Jains, Parsis and Christians. Furthermore, this exclusion applies only to persons from three of India's neighbouring countries—Pakistan, Bangladesh and Afghanistan. The Statement of Objects and Reasons (SOR) of the Citizenship Bill 2019 focuses on benefitting 'persecuted minorities' from the above three countries whose state religion is Islam.

> 2. It is a historical fact that trans-border migration of population has been happening continuously between the territories of India and the areas presently comprised in Pakistan, Afghanistan and Bangladesh. Millions

---

[111] ibid.
[112] ibid.

of citizens of undivided India belonging to various faiths were staying in the said areas of Pakistan and Bangladesh when India was partitioned in 1947. The constitutions of Pakistan, Afghanistan and Bangladesh provide for a specific state religion. As a result, many persons belonging to Hindu, Sikh, Buddhist, Jain, Parsi and Christian communities have faced persecution on grounds of religion in those countries. Some of them also have fears about such persecution in their day-to-day life where right to practice, profess and propagate their religion has been obstructed and restricted. Many such persons have fled to India to seek shelter and continued to stay in India even if their travel documents have expired or they have incomplete or no documents. 3. Under the existing provisions of the Act, migrants from Hindu, Sikh, Buddhist, Jain, Parsi or Christian communities from Afghanistan, Pakistan or Bangladesh who entered into India without valid travel documents or if the validity of their documents has expired are regarded as illegal migrants and ineligible to apply for Indian citizenship under section 5 or section 6 of the Act.[113]

Curiously, the SOR seems to have telescoped time, seeming to give an impression that we are closer in time to 1947 when Partition took place. Furthermore, agnostics and atheists do not seem to figure in the category of persecuted persons. It is far from clear and there seems some reason for not disclosing the total number of applicants for citizenship in the category concerned and how long they have been waiting. Some people

---

[113] Statements of Objects and Reasons, Citizenship Amendment Bill, 2019.

suggest that the number is not more than 30,000. But then, over the years, several thousand have been given citizenship under the parent legislation and those include Muslims. Why others of Indian origin did not make it is not known.

It is perplexing how Parliament believes that the persecuted minorities in the above-mentioned countries do not include the 'Muslim' population. It is presumed that since they live in countries that recognize 'Islam' as its state religion, they are sheltered from atrocities by their governments on grounds of religion, which is inflicted on 'other minorities'. However, in Balochistan, which is one of the four provinces of Pakistan, the Baloch, along with Pashtuns and Brahuis (Muslims), are politically and economically marginalized. They have been subject to a heavy-handed armed response by the Pakistani government, time and again, for demanding more provincial autonomy to escape exploitative central nationalist policies. This form of persecution, which has seen thousands of deaths due to violence by state actors, has been noticed globally as a conflict that needs resolution. A 2006 report by the Human Rights Commission of Pakistan brought to light the insurgencies, detention, torture, extra-judicial and summary executions, disappearances, etc., against the Baloch, corroborated by Amnesty International.[114] The Baloch are thus left to suffer, with little to no support from neighbouring countries, especially India, who by virtue of the CAA would not recognize them as 'persecuted', and a natural bar imposed through the exclusion

---

[114] 'How Balochistan became a part of Pakistan – a historical perspective', available at: https://nation.com.pk/05-Dec-2015/how-balochistan-became-a-part-of-pakistan-a-historical-perspective. Last accessed on 22 February 2020.

of 'Muslims' from the amendment. Curiously, this is so despite the Prime Minister having vowed his support to Balochistan from the ramparts of the Red Fort. Interestingly, Khan Abdul Ghaffar Khan or the Frontier Gandhi, a proud Pashtun who spent long years in Pakistani prisons, would not have qualified for Indian citizenship under the CAA.

Curiously, the CAA was preceded by the 2015 amendment of the Foreigners Order, 1948, whereby the newly inserted Rule 3A exempted persons belonging to minority communities in Bangladesh and Pakistan (namely Hindus, Sikhs, Buddhists, Jains, Parsis and Christians) who were compelled to seek shelter in India due to religious persecution or fear of the same on or before 31 December 2014, from the Foreigners Act, 1946. It would be noted that Afghanistan was not included at that stage. It is a moot point as to why this preparatory step towards CAA went unnoticed and unchallenged.

Similar is the case for Ahmadiyyas in Pakistan who have been persecuted by the Sunni majority population for believing in Mirza Gulam Ahmad to be the promised Messiah. In a country that has a state religion, Ahmadiyyas are precluded from being recognized as Muslims according to the Pakistani Constitution, effectively making them a minority group. Article 260 of the Constitution of Pakistan was amended with effect from 17 September 1974 to define Muslims to the exclusion of 'Ahmadiyyas'. It reads as:

Article 260[115]

(a) 'Muslim' means a person who believes in the unity and oneness of Almighty Allah, in the absolute and

---

[115] Article 260, Constitution of Pakistan.

unqualified finality of the Prophethood of Muhammad (peace be upon him), the last of the prophets, and does not believe in, or recognize as a prophet or religious reformer, any person who claimed or claims to be a prophet, in any sense of the word or of any description whatsoever, after Muhammad (peace be upon him);

(b) 'non-Muslim' means a person who is not a Muslim and includes a person belonging to the Christian, Hindu, Sikh, Buddhist or Parsi community, a person of the Quadiani group or the Lahori group (who call themselves Ahmadis or by any other name), or a Bahai, and a person belonging to any of the scheduled castes.

This constitutional de-recognition of Ahmadiyyas from the definition of 'Muslims' and the prevailing anti-Ahmadiyya sentiment in the majority population has resulted in large-scale violence and persecution. The 1953 Lahore riots and the 1974 anti-Ahmadiyya riots are stark reminders of their persecution in a country which has, perhaps, their largest population in the world. Additionally, in 2018, anti-blasphemy laws were introduced by the Pakistani government which are supplemental to Ordinance XX, introduced in 1984 to bar public practice of their faith, use of honorific titles, etc., as punishable with imprisonment.

It has also been debated that the non-inclusion of minorities from other neighbouring countries, particularly from Sri Lanka or even Bhutan, is illogical. In Sri Lanka, thousands of Tamils faced discrimination and violence at the hands of the majoritarian Sinhalese, in a civil war that lasted more than two decades and culminated in the horrific massacre of Liberation Tigers of Tamil Eelam (LTTE) cadres. These excluded Hindus (Tamils) who have been at the receiving end of state-led atrocities and ethnically targeted and isolated in Sri Lanka. People who follow Buddhism in Sri Lanka had also been radicalized, leading to the formation of violent groups. If an assumption of 'having roots in India' is to be made for the purposes of the benefits of CAA, Sri Lankan Hindu Tamils would definitely form part as indeed Sikhs from Afghanistan, but not because of religious persecution in their case.

Historically speaking, the Third Anglo-Afghan War ultimately ended the British pursuit of colonizing Afghanistan. The Afghans retained their independence and were officially recognized as sovereign by the British. Having had a tumultuous relationship with the Taliban with elements of Pakistani ISI and military conflicts with the erstwhile Soviet Union and the US, Afghanistan is a country of persecuted citizens, irrespective of the status of its citizens as majority and minority. The relationship of Afghanistan with India thus remains merely geopolitical. In such a case, where the Partition of India did not lead to an exodus of migrants to either side, including the minority population of Afghanistan in the CAA is stretching the description a bit but seems to explain the late inclusion.

Nepal, Bhutan, Myanmar, etc., are countries (and Tibet as an autonomous region of China) that have seen disturbances and persecution of a section of the populace over a period of time. Having given refuge to His Holiness, The Dalai Lama and his followers; to the hundreds of Nepalis crossing the border every day for economic gains; condemning the Myanmar government for its treatment of the Rohingyas on international platforms; and advocating the cause of Hindu Lhotsampas from Bhutan and Urdu-speaking people from Bangladesh (victims of persecution based on language and culture), etc., India should definitely have thought through the geopolitical consequences of such a law.

What is 'persecution' and particularly 'religious persecution' thus begs the question. Curiously, although persecution is mentioned in the SOR of the amendment, the statutory text does not refer to it. Why then was this law passed? Who does it truly protect if so many of the 'persecuted' are left out? The SOR along with its provisions refrains from going into the definition of 'persecution' or 'refugee'. Interestingly, India is not even a signatory to the convention relating to the status of refugees, also known as the Refugee Convention, 1951. Indeterminacy in the UNHCR as regards the interpretation of 'persecution' still leaves the term to be understood as widely as can be. Such an interpretation could be gleaned from Articles 1A and 33 of the Convention.[116]

> Article 1. Definition of the term 'refugee' A. For the purposes of the present Convention, the term 'refugee' shall apply to any person who:
>
> (1) Has been considered a refugee under the Arrangements of 12 May 1926 and 30 June 1928 or under the Conventions of 28 October 1933 and 10

---

[116] Convention relating to the Status of Refugees Adopted on 28 July 1951 by the United Nations Conference of Plenipotentiaries on the Status of Refugees and Stateless Persons convened under General Assembly resolution 429 (V) of 14 December 1950 Entry into force: 22 April 1954, in accordance with Article 43.

February 1938, the Protocol of 14 September 1939 or the Constitution of the International Refugee Organization; Decisions of non-eligibility taken by the International Refugee Organization during the period of its activities shall not prevent the status of refugee being accorded to persons who fulfil the conditions of paragraph 2 of this section;

(2) As a result of events occurring before 1 January 1951 and owing to well-founded fear of being persecuted for reasons of race, religion, nationality, membership of a particular social group or political opinion, is outside the country of his nationality and is unable or, owing to such fear, is unwilling to avail himself of the protection of that country; or who, not having a nationality and being outside the country of his former habitual residence as a result of such events, is unable or, owing to such fear, is unwilling to return to it. In the case of a person who has more than one nationality, the term 'the country of his nationality' shall mean each of the countries of which he is a national, and a person shall not be deemed to be lacking the protection of the country of his nationality if, without any valid reason based on well-founded fear, he has not availed himself of the protection of one of the countries of which he is a national.

Article 33. Prohibition of expulsion or return ('refoulement')

1. No Contracting State shall expel or return ('refouler') a refugee in any manner whatsoever to the frontiers of territories where his life or freedom would be

threatened on account of his race, religion, nationality, membership of a particular social group or political opinion.

2. The benefit of the present provision may not, however, be claimed by a refugee whom there are reasonable grounds for regarding as a danger to the security of the country in which he is, or who, having been convicted by a final judgement of a particularly serious crime, constitutes a danger to the community of that country.

These provisions read with Article 14 of the Universal Declaration of Human Rights would essentially indicate that any group of people, which has a well-grounded fear of safety from state-actors, in their State of Origin (or where they reside habitually) on grounds of race, religion, nationality, membership of a social group or political opinion will be deemed to be persecuted.

Article 14[117]

1. Everyone has the right to seek and to enjoy in other countries asylum from persecution.
2. This right may not be invoked in the case of prosecutions genuinely arising from non-political crimes or from acts contrary to the purposes and principles of the United Nations.

What needs to be pointed out here is that when this Convention came into effect, it established a rather broad category of people by indicating the mental state of refugees. Terror of persecution, anxiety and misgivings are all subjective

---

[117] Article 14, Universal Declaration of Human Rights, 1948.

requirements to show 'well-founded fear'. It could signify 'actual' or 'future possibility' of persecution.[118] Doctrinal developments[119] along with administrative and judicial case laws on refugee, in their interpretation of 'persecution', have indicated the use of human rights to define the core principles of 'Who is a victim? Who carries out persecution? When is it carried out?' and so on.

Physical, psychological and economic persecutions are standard categories for interpretation. It varies from murder and torture to separation from family, prejudicial economic policies aimed at a group and even proselytization.

The CAA, in its implicit endeavour to subsume a refugee law in its Citizenship Act, has forgotten to give concrete rationale for inclusion of only a few religious groups or countries given the broad contours of persecution.

Border states such as Assam and Tripura have raised serious opposition to the CAA on larger issues than just religion. The Liberation War of 1971 forced millions of citizens to escape the civil war between East and West Pakistan which was genocidal in nature. Mass illegal migrations to Assam, West Bengal and other parts of India to seek refuge turned into grabbing of local resources by the migrants, adding more fuel to the Assam Movement (1979–85). The Assamese felt that their indigenous culture and ethos were threatened by the huge influx of Bangladeshi immigrants, both Hindus and Muslims.

---

[118] N. Robinson, *Convention Relating to the Status of Refugees – its history, contents and interpretation.* Institute of Jewish Affairs, New York, 1953, p. 48.

[119] José H. Fischel De Andrade, 'On the Development of the Concept of "Persecution" in International Refugee Law. *III. Anuário Brasileiro De Direito Internacional*, 3(2), p. 126.

Vast stretches of open border with Bangladesh and ineffective implementation of the Immigration (expulsion from Assam) Act, 1950, led to a NRC of Assam as under the 1951 Census. The idea of the NRC was to prepare a list of all documents and particulars of every single person living in Assam at the time, village-wise. Number and names of persons, parents' names, houses or holdings belonging to them, nationality, age, etc., were among the many particulars indicated therein. This was to be done under the directive issued by the Ministry of Home Affairs. Time and again, through each census conducted, promises were made by the Central Government to the state of Assam to conduct and implement the NRC speedily and issue national identity cards, but it was a policy lost in translation. The frustration with the Government of India and the influx of illegal migrants led to what we know as the Assam Movement. The Assam Movement saw large-scale violence, especially the Khoirabari massacre of 1983 (against Bengali Hindu immigrants) and the Nellie massacre (against Bengali Muslims). The government's efforts to resonate with the masses and find peace bore fruit in the signing of the Assam Accord between AASU, All Assam Gana Sangram Parishad and the Government of India on 15 August 1985.

The Assam Accord provided for 1 January 1966 as its base date and year for identifying foreigners. Those who came prior to the base date and whose names appeared in the electoral rolls of 1967 were to be regularized. Foreigners who came after 1 January 1966 and up to 24 March 1971 were to be detected and deleted from the electoral rolls, all in accordance with the Foreigners Act, 1946 and Foreigners (Tribunals) Order, 1964. The triple D (detect, delete and deport) method was to be followed to identify foreigners who would then have to register themselves under Registration of Foreigners Act, 1939 and Registration of Foreigners Rules, 1939.[120] Accordingly, those detected were to be deleted from electoral rolls for 10 years from the date of detection. While those who came after 25 March 1971, were to be immediately put under the triple D process. To be able to sort the difficulties faced by individuals and yet identify illegal immigrants for deportation, the Illegal Migrants (Determination by Tribunals) Act, 1983 (hereinafter IMDT Act) was passed to expel illegal Bangladeshi migrants from the state who had cast a heavy burden on the state's resources and undermined its cultural integrity.

Section 6A, Citizenship Act, 1955, inserted consequent to the Assam Accord distinguished persons of Indian origin (those who were born or whose either parents or grandparents were born in undivided India) from persons 'detected to be a foreigner'. This statutory clarity reinforced the triple D process with much vigour, especially in the context of the Persons of Indian Origin (PIO), as discussed below

Restoration of normalcy, socio-economic development of Assam and specific complaints relating to Indian Citizenship Certificates (ICC) was to be looked into. The NRC was to be updated by conducting fresh scrutiny and the illegal immigrants were to be sent back, but the government agencies found it to be a herculean task, and were unable to neutralize the tension in Assam. In the meantime, the Central Government made an amendment to the Citizenship Act, 1955, by inserting Section 6A, made especially for the state of Assam in tandem with the Assam Accord.

---

[120] Rule 5.3, Assam Accord, 1985.

Section 6A[121]—Special provisions as to citizenship of persons covered by the Assam Accord.

(1) For the purposes of this section—
- (a) 'Assam' means the territories included in the State of Assam immediately before the commencement of the Citizenship (Amendment) Act, 1985;
- (b) 'detected to be a foreigner' means detected to be a foreigner in accordance with the provisions of the Foreigners Act, 1946 (31 of 1946) and the Foreigners (Tribunals) Order, 1964 by a Tribunal constituted under the said Order;
- (c) 'specified territory' means the territories included in Bangladesh immediately before the commencement of the Citizenship (Amendment) Act, 1985;
- (d) a person shall be deemed to be of Indian origin, if he, or either of his parents for any of his grandparents was born in undivided India;
- (e) a person shall be deemed to have been detected to be a foreigner on the date on which a Tribunal constituted under the Foreigners (Tribunals) Order, 1964 submits its opinion to the effect that he is a foreigner to the officer or authority concerned.

(2) Subject to the provisions of sub-sections (6) and (7), all persons of Indian origin who came before the 1st day of January, 1966 to Assam from the specified territory (including such of those whose names were

---

[121] Ins. By Act 65 of 1985, sec 2 (w.e.f 7-12-1985), Citizenship Act, 1955.

included in the electoral rolls used for the purposes of the General Election to the House of the People held in 1967) and who have been ordinarily resident in Assam since the dates of their entry into Assam shall be deemed to be citizens of India as from the 1st day of January, 1966.

(3) Subject to the provisions of sub-sections (6) and (7), every person of Indian origin who—
   (a) came to Assam on or after the lst day of January 1966 but before the 25th day of March 1971 from the specified territory; and
   (b) has, since the date of his entry into Assam, been ordinarily resident in Assam; and
   (c) has been detected to be a foreigner, shall register himself in accordance with the rules made by the Central Government in this behalf under section 18 with such authority (thereafter in this sub-section referred to as the registering authority) as may be specified in such rules and if his name is included in any electoral roll for any Assembly or Parliamentary constituency in force on the date of such detection, his name shall be deleted there from.

Explanation.—In the case of every person seeking registration under this sub-section, the opinion of the Tribunal constituted under the Foreigners (Tribunals) Order, 1964 holding such person to be a foreigner, shall be deemed to be sufficient proof of the requirement under clause (c) of this sub-section and if any question arises as to whether such person complies with any other requirement under this sub-section, the registering authority shall,—

(i) if such opinion contains a finding with respect to such other requirement, decide the question in conformity with such finding;

(ii) if such opinion does not contain a finding with respect to such other requirement, refer the question to a Tribunal constituted under the said Order hang jurisdiction in accordance with such rules as the Central Government may make in this behalf under section 18 and decide the question in conformity with the opinion received on such reference.

(4) A person registered under sub-section (3) shall have, as from the date on which he has been detected to be a foreigner and till the expiry of a period of ten years from that date, the same rights and obligations as a citizen of India (including the right to obtain a passport under the Passports Act, 1967 (15 of 1967) and the obligations connected therewith), but shall not be entitled to have his name included in any electoral roll for any Assembly or Parliamentary constituency at any time before the expiry of the said period of ten years.

(5) A person registered under sub-section (3) shall be deemed to be a citizen of India for all purposes as from the date of expiry of a period of ten years from the date on which he has been detected to be a foreigner.

(6) Without prejudice to the provisions of section 8, —

(a) If any person referred to in sub-section (2)

submits in the prescribed manner and form and to the prescribed authority within sixty days from the date of commencement of the Citizenship (Amendment) Act, 1985, for year a declaration that he does not wish to be a citizen of India, such person shall not be deemed to have become a citizen of India under that sub-section;

(b) If any person referred to in sub-section (3) submits in the prescribed manner and form and to the prescribed authority within sixty days from the date of commencement the Citizenship (Amendment) Act, 1985, for year or from the date on which he has been detected to be a foreigner, whichever is later, a declaration that he does not wish to be governed by the provisions of that sub-section and sub-sections (4) and (5), it shall not be necessary for such person to register himself under sub-section (3).

Explanation.—Where a person required to file a declaration under this sub-section does not have the capacity to enter into a contract, such declaration may be filed on his behalf by any person competent under the law for the time being in force to act on his behalf.

(7) Nothing in sub-sections (2) to (6) shall apply in relation to any person—
  (a) who, immediately before the commencement of the Citizenship (Amendment) Act, 1985, for year is a citizen of India;
  (b) who was expelled from India before the commencement of the Citizenship (Amendment)

Act, 1985, for year under the Foreigners Act, 1946 (31 of 1946).

(8) Save as otherwise expressly provided in this section, the provisions of this section shall have effect notwithstanding anything contained in any other law for the time being in force.

This section brought more clarity to the procedure enumerated in the Assam Accord. Save from reiteration as regards procedure for those detected to be a foreigner, this section also dealt with people who came to India after 1 January 1966 but before 25 March 1971. Under sub-section (2), such persons who were detected to be foreigners were to register themselves under Section 18, Citizenship Act, 1955, which provided the Central Government with power to make rules in respect of registration procedures, etc. Sub-section (3) of Section 6A provided for every person of 'Indian Origin' who came in the time period mentioned above who sought to get registered with the registration authority to get the benefits of a citizen of India. Any findings of the Tribunal as to rendering of an opinion for 'deeming the person to be a foreigner' would be considered as 'sufficient proof'. In case of any question with regards to conformity with any other requirements, the registering authority could render an opinion itself or refer the question to the Tribunal (Order 1964) and then act on such reference. The section mandated a 10-year period post-detection to enable the person to benefit from all rights that an Indian citizen has except voting (or being registered in the electoral roll). This was done to confirm determination of residency de facto, in India. Post the expiry of these 10 years, the concerned persons would be 'deemed to be a citizen'. This amended section also provided these people with the option to opt out of gaining Indian citizenship by filing a declaration directly or by a competent person on their behalf, to the concerned authority within 60 days of commencement of the amendment Act. There is little information of any such declarations. But huge anecdotal and documented data is available of family members being torn apart on the basis of NRC.

Assam Sanmilita Mahasangha, which has challenged the validity of Section 6A of the Citizenship Act, 1955, in the Supreme Court, maintained that the publication of the updated NRC, without disposing of its petition, would create a 'clumsy' situation in the state. Section 6A, the result of the 1985 Assam Accord, prescribes 24 March 1971, as the cut-off date for detection and deportation of illegal migrants and accordingly, the NRC is being updated in the state with the same cut-off date. This matter is referred to the Constitution Bench but has not been heard for four years.

Lt. General S.K. Sinha, the then governor of Assam, submitted an extensive report[122] on the adverse impact these illegal migrations had on the indigenous tribes of Assam who were being reduced to a minority in their own state. Giving historical perspective on this migration, he pointed out:

1. Illegal migration from Bangladesh into Assam should be viewed against the backdrop of past history, present realities and future designs. Migration into Assam has been taking place from the dawn of history. However, after the British annexed Assam, large scale population

---

[122] Lt. Gen (Retd) S.K. Sinha, 'Report on Illegal Migrations into Assam', available at: https://jagadishbhuyan.in/downloads/SK%20Sinha%27s%20REPORT.pdf. Last accessed on 25 March 2020.

movement from the South (Bengal, East Pakistan and now Bangladesh) has been an ongoing phenomenon for over a century. Initially, this movement was for economic reasons only but with the approach of Independence, it started developing both communal and political overtones. After Independence, it acquired an international dimension and it now poses a grave threat to our national security.

2. The British developed the tea industry in Assam. They imported labour from Bihar and other provinces to work in the tea gardens. The Assamese people living mostly in Upper Assam and cultivating one crop per year, were not interested in working as labour in the tea gardens nor in increasing or expanding land cultivation to meet the additional requirement of food for the large labour population employed in the tea gardens. Therefore, the British encouraged Bengali Muslim peasants from present Bangladesh to move into Lower Assam for putting virgin land under cultivation. This set-in motion a movement pattern which despite changed conditions, has been continuing to this day.

3. The Assamese fear of losing their identity and being swamped by Bengalis goes back to this merger and even earlier. This fear had been aroused both by the Bengali Hindus dominating the administration and the professions, and the Bengali Muslims altering the demography of the province. The Bengali Muslims were hard working peasants who occupied vacant land and put virgin areas under cultivation. They made a significant contribution to the agricultural economy of Assam.

Sinha also pointed out the conflicting viewpoints as regards the triple D measure discussed above by stating:

> Measures to stem illegal migration can be undertaken without any controversy but any alternation of status quo in regard to detection and deportation of these migrants will result in strident assertion of conflicting viewpoints. The 'secular' parties and the minorities do not see any danger from illegal migration. They believe that most of the so-called illegal migrants are Bengali speaking Indian Muslims and this issue has been unnecessarily blown out of proportion. They fear that in the garb of deporting foreigners, Indian Muslims will be harassed. Thus, they are for the continuance of IMDT Act in its present form. On the other hand, the majority community of Assam and the political parties dubbed as 'communal' by the 'secularists' have a diametrically opposite viewpoint. They are gravely concerned about the large influx of illegal migrants and want their ingress stopped. They also want that the highly discriminating IMDT Act be repealed forthwith. There appears to be no meeting ground between these opposing views. Notwithstanding this, it is in our national interest to work out a mutually acceptable solution to this burning problem, which not only affects the people of Assam but the entire nation.'

Sinha suggested measures to curb this problem through border fencing, registering the national boats plying in the river near the border, effective arrangements for registration of births and deaths, raising awareness among the people not only about indigenous tribes but also about the threat to national security,

NRC to be updated and computerized while a special register should be maintained for stateless persons.

The NRC remained a work in progress, hoping to see the light of day. However, administrative hurdles and political hesitations, among many other constraints, make it a real challenge to overcome.

In the meantime, Assam saw growing dissatisfaction with the implementation of the IMDT Act, 1983 and the modest record of persons identified. A writ petition was filed in the Supreme Court of India in the year 2000 by the current chief minister of Assam, Sarbananda Sonowal,[123] challenging the constitutionality of the IMDT Act, which was Assam-specific. The Act gave innumerable benefits to illegal migrants in the following ways. Section 3 defined an illegal migrant as a person having entered India on or after 25 March 1971 without valid documents as required by law. Those who entered India before this date, however, were to be governed by the Foreigners Act. Section 8 provided for opportunity to illegal migrants to make a representation to the Tribunal if aggrieved by its order. This was a special privilege accorded to them that no other foreigner could get under any existing law. In addition to these, the IMDT Act was silent on the aspect of burden of proof which essentially cast a very heavy burden on the state authorities to establish that the person concerned was, in fact, an illegal migrant and was liable to be deported. Perjury charges against citizens (claiming existence of illegal migrants) if contents are found to be false in the form, no right of appeal against rejection of application by authority under the Act, requirement of affidavit by citizens situated in the

---

[123] Sarbananda Sonowal vs Union of India (2005) 5 SCC 665.

jurisdiction of the police station where migrant is found, etc., were provisions ineffective to contain what was described as an invasion-like situation in the Northeast. Thus, the Supreme Court lay the matter to rest by holding that the object of the Act was defeated. Instead of deporting the illegal migrants, the IMDT sought to cast a heavy burden of proof on the state which also violated Article 355 of the Constitution in as much as the Union protecting the state of Assam from infiltration and threat to internal security is concerned. The lack of a rational nexus between the object of the Act and its classification also violated Article 14 of the Constitution holding the IMDT Act, in conclusion, as ultra vires.

The NRC was included in the Citizenship Act, 1955, by the 2003 amendment to the Act. Section 14A provided for the Union Government to issue national identity cards to all citizens and to maintain a national register with records of all citizens of India. The purpose was to weed out those who were residing in India illegally. However, Assam witnessed a rather tumultuous period of riots till 2013 that halted this process. With anger at not being able to fulfil the promises set out in the Assam Accord, a writ petition was filed in the Supreme Court by Assam Sanmilita Mahasangha.[124] The Supreme Court ordered that an NRC be conducted in Assam and be finally published by 2016.

The updated final list for the State of Assam was released in 2019. This verification of citizenship ended up excluding approximately 19 lakh people who could then appeal to the Foreigners Tribunals to seek an appropriate order. Contrary to the expectations of political parties that were aggressively pushing the NRC process, the final list threw up a larger

---

[124] Assam Sanmilita Mahasangha vs Union of India, 2015 (3) SCC 1.

number of Bengali Hindus than their Muslim counterparts. Strenuous efforts to persuade the Supreme Court to direct fresh scrutiny were unsuccessful.

Section 6B that was introduced in the CAA 2019, abates any pending proceedings against illegal migrants in the Foreigners Tribunals who belong to any of the six religions: Hindu, Sikh, Jain, Parsi, Christian and Buddhist. This section also states that nothing will apply to areas falling under the Sixth Schedule of the Constitution and areas under the Inner Line Permit.

The problem, however, arises in the fact that there are only 10 autonomous districts in Assam, Meghalaya, Mizoram and Tripura that fall under the Sixth Schedule. Only these districts will gain the benefit of exemption of the amendment, that is, all illegal migrants who by virtue of the amendment are eligible to be citizens (belonging to any of the six mentioned religions) will not be allowed to settle in these areas. The remainder areas in these states will have to grant all citizenship-related rights to these migrants, which defeats the purpose of protecting the states from influx of migrants, generally. As pointed out earlier, the north-eastern states are affected by internal security threats which the court said was equivalent to external aggression.[125]

With the new law coming in, NRC and CAA will have to be read together because, of the 19 lakh excluded from the final list, a large percentage will receive the benefit from belonging to any of the six religions under the CAA and will automatically become citizens.

The problem is quite simple, at least in the context of Assam. The entire state is up in arms about outsiders irrespective of religion. The Central Government is seen

---

[125] Sarbananda Sonowal vs Union of India (2005) 5 SCC 665, Para 63.

as giving to all outsiders, excluding Muslims, the right to become citizens and reside anywhere in India and use the country's limited resources, to the detriment of the pre-existing 138 crore people in India. This addition of people to the population and a compromised economic policy in its current shape will only go on to add burden on the State Exchequer. In Assam's context, once people from the six religions are identified and granted the status of citizens, there will be no bar to their stay in any other part of Assam that is not covered under the Sixth Schedule. This, in their view, clearly defeats the purpose of NRC in Assam and the objectives of the Assam Accord.

Nationwide implementation of NRC with its baseline date of 31 December 2014, as promised by the current regime, is a perceived threat to the Muslim community who have been excluded from the benefits of the new amendment. There are many potholes in conducting an exercise such as this, to the exclusion of one religious community. India is a vast developing country with a weak institutional framework. A large chunk of the poor may not have documents to verify their religion or their citizenship status as the NRC and CAA would together demand. While people professing any of the the six religions as mentioned in the CAA will gain from not being deported, most Muslims without documents (when the NRC is conducted nationwide) would find themselves at the mercy of the Foreigners Tribunals and the detention centres. The Central Government reiterates at multiple rallies that the existing Muslims in India have nothing to worry about. But does that include those Muslims that have no verification documents and have been living in India for years, let alone generations?

It has been suggested that the NPR, which was first used in 2010 by the UPA government for PDS and other welfare benefits, be updated from April 2020. NPR's purpose is to include all those who 'reside' in India. Residents in the context of NPR is understood to mean those who have been residing in India for the last six months or have the intention of doing so. It records only demographic data such as place of residence, duration, parents' names, nationality (as declared), etc. While the NPR is only to record proof of residence, NRC is to record proof of citizenship and to detain/deport those who are not citizens.

The NPR is prepared at the local (village/subtown), subdistrict, district, state and national levels under provisions of the Citizenship Act, 1955, and the Citizenship (Registration of Citizens and Issue of National Identity Cards) Rules, 2003. Essentially, it is similar to the Family Register that is kept at the panchayat level. Every person residing at a place for six months or more is required to register and give 15 points of information. It was last updated in 2010 (and rejigged with Aadhaar card data in 2015) and will be repeated in 2020. Doubts have arisen because of the impression that this time round, information will be sought on the date and place of birth of the individuals' parents and grandparents. The exercise is done in parallel with the house-listing phase of the Census. The next step is presumed to be the proposed NRC that will segregate citizens from foreigners based on the account of the verified NPR to show doubtful persons. It is being assumed that non-Muslims will be able to fall back on the CAA for reclaiming citizenship status, but Muslims will not get that benefit. It is another matter that all beneficiaries of the CAA would have already submitted their affidavits that they are Indian citizens and in any case, will have precious little information on any alleged persecution in the three mentioned countries.

The Home Minister of India, in December 2019, had said

that chronologically, the NPR will come first and then the NRC will be conducted nationwide. He had defended the nationwide NRC by saying that it was needed to weed out 'all illegal infiltrators' from India. Incidentally, after a few days, the Prime Minister denied any such nationwide registration by suggesting the lack of discussion on the same. There has, however, not been any indication by the current regime rejecting pan-India NRC. The Citizenship (Registration of Citizens and Issue of National Identity Cards) Rules, 2003 provides for both registration of citizens (NRC) and population register (NPR under Rule 2). This indicates the possible use of NPR in the NRC exercise which has been denied by the Home Minister. The government has insisted that the use of NPR is restricted to understanding the demography, but its purpose is unclear with an existing Census programme. At best, the NPR can be used as a mechanism to identify the residents and when put together with the NRC and CAA, make it easy to exclude the Muslim 'illegal infiltrators' since the other 'migrants' stand to benefit on account of belonging to one of the specified religions.

This matter is now pending judgement in the Supreme Court but at the outset, the CAA and NRC are seen by many as unreasonable and discriminatory political agenda. If the CAA is upheld by the Supreme Court, several lakh of persons in Assam and an unimaginable number from the rest of the country will have to be deported, to where no one knows. Alternatively, they will have the unedifying choice of life in detention centres or becoming disenfranchised lesser citizens.

Documents Define Identity

For several years, the Central Government and Assam dragged their feet on implementing the NRC, presumably anticipating the difficulties that could arise. However, the Supreme Court (Justice Ranjan Gogoi as his Lordship then was and later as Chief Justice sitting with Justice Rohinton Nariman) took matters under its control and closely monitored the proceed; the NRC for the state of Assam had 14 documents in list A and eight in list B described as legacy and link documents. Any one of the documents from either list could be used as proof of citizenship. In the Assam NRC, it was required to show lineage documents with 25 March 1971 as the cut-off date. Those who could not provide their linkage with the cut-off date were per force excluded. If a pan-India NRC takes place, the cut-off date will be 31 December 2014. Does that mean lack of being able to establish lineage strips a person of citizenship, just as in Assam that left out 19 lakh people? The experience of Assam is a pointer to seemingly insurmountable problems, like young women shifting their residence upon marriage.

Having said this, India is a large country with a majority of its population poor and illiterate. Documentation thus becomes a herculean task not only for the authorities conducting this exercise but also for the people to own them. Geographical factors such as cyclones (in coastal areas), floods due to heavy monsoon or change in the course of the rivers, earthquakes, internal migration and so on, contribute to loss of property, documents and family trees.

Documents can have wide-ranging problems—from having spelt the name or surname of the person or parents inaccurately to an outdated address or photo ID, apart from loss and destruction. Birth certificates are procured and filed with much difficulty, as can be seen from the problems in introduction of welfare schemes by the government. Bureaucratic hurdles in the form of lack of cooperation by officials surveying the documents and declaring some profiles as 'doubtful' create a perception of fear and uncertainty. The consequence of such unreliability in documentation does not, unfortunately, give the excluded or doubtful any mitigation. Once deemed to be an illegal migrant due to lack of proof of citizenship, the concerned person has the right to appeal to the Foreigners Tribunals but with a reversed burden. Furthermore, many may not have the money to file claims of appeals against their exclusion from the NRC, thereby subjecting them to the horrors of detention centres and statelessness!

There is still no clarity on the documents to be relied on to prove one's citizenship except the Assam precedent. The Supreme Court, in 2003, had reiterated its legal position[126] on documents marked as exhibits and their proof as being distinct. Merely producing documents and marking them as exhibits will not be tantamount to proof of its contents. It will need to be vouched for, by persons in accordance with the law, to be admissible.

---

[126] Narbada Devi Gupta vs Birendra Kumar Jaiswal, (2003) 8 SSC 745.

In the case of Md. Babul Islam,[127] the Guwahati High Court had held that electoral photo identity card (EPIC) is not sufficient proof of citizenship, in the absence of any supporting evidence. On 12 February 2020,[128] the Guwahati High Court examined the Foreigners Tribunals' order and upheld it on grounds of not being able to prove conclusively his residence in Assam prior to 25 March 1971. The petitioner had shown five documents: EPIC, registered sale deeds of 1964 and 1970, revenue receipt of 1971, and the voter list of 1997 bearing his name. The High Court reiterated his failure to show documents such as voter list prior to 1997 and insisted that sale deeds, being private documents, need to be supplemented in accordance with the Narbada Devi principle. This principle lays down the need for contents of the documents to be proved or vouched for by litigants in court when used as exhibits. On the same day, a different bench held Jabeda Begum[129] to be a foreigner by disregarding her PAN card, bank documents and land tax receipts as insufficient evidence.

On 17 February 2020, the Guwahati High Court declared a 42-year-old woman, Sahera Khatun,[130] a foreigner, confirming the Tribunals' order. She had shown 14 documents to the court, including a school certificate (where she studied till class 1 in 1986), marriage certificate and voter lists of 1966, 1970, 1977, 2005 and 2017 containing the names of her parents, grandparents and siblings. The court held that Sahera Khatun was unable to connect herself to her projected parents, grandparents, etc., in any other list by means of a cogent,

---

[127] Md. Babul Islam vs State of Assam, WP (C) No. 3547/2016.
[128] Munindra Biswas vs Union of India, WP (C) No. 7426/2019.
[129] Jabeda Khatun vs Union of India, WP (C) No. 7451/2019.
[130] Sahera Khatun vs Union of India, WP (C) No. 7482/2019.

reliable and admissible evidence. The statement given by her brother was not considered since it could not be proven in court that they indeed were siblings. Her school certificate was not confirmed, as it lacked the support of the headmaster's testimony and her mother's absence during cross-examination led the court to hold her as a foreigner.

Similarly, on 28 February 2020, the Guwahati High Court, in Rabia Khatun's case,[131] held that while the electoral roll of 1965 reflected her grandfather's name, none of the list of voters exhibited her name along with his, making her claim unreliable. Since her name was not listed alongside her grandfather's, the proof of relationship between them was questioned. Additionally, her marriage certificate was not proved through the legal testimony of the issuing authority, making it inadmissible as proof of citizenship.

What is even more baffling is the conflict between the Additional Chief Metropolitan Magistrate, Esplanade Court, Mumbai, and the Guwahati High Court as regards evidentiary value of Voter ID or EPIC. While the Guwahati High Court has consistently held (as mentioned earlier) that the EPIC is not a valid proof of citizenship in itself, the Mumbai court in its judgement[132] on 11 February 2020, held the EPIC to be valid since it is issued under a declaration filed with the Election Commission of India with punishment for a false claim.

> It is necessary to note that the Aadhaar card, PAN card, driving licence or ration card cannot be termed as the documents proving the citizenship of any person in a

---

[131] Rabia Khatun vs Union of India, WP (C) No. 6369/2019.
[132] Abbas Lalmiya Shaikh and Rabiyakhatun Abbas Shaikh, C. C. No. 352/PW/2017.

sufficient manner as said documents are not meant for the purpose of citizenship. The birth certificate, domicile certificate, bonafide certificate, passport, etc., can be relied upon to establish the origin of any person. Even the election card can be said to be sufficient proof of citizenship as while applying for the election card or voting card, a person has to file declaration with the authority in view of Form 6 of Peoples Representation Act to the authority that he is a citizen of India and if the declaration is found false, he is liable for punishment. To my mind such a declaration is sufficient to prove the citizenship unless contrary is proved by the prosecution. Here, it is visible that accused no. 2 and accused no. 3 have filed their original election cards on record. It is not the case of prosecution that the accused no. 2 and 3 have prepared fake documents.

The Central Government, with the CAA and the intention of conducting a pan-India NRC, should have given it a deeper thought to finalize what documents they want shown! With this lack of clarity in the 'Show Your Documents' drive, a large number of people get sent to detention camps, with no concrete treaty with countries such as Bangladesh for deporting migrants.

The legal basis for detention centres in India is indicated in the Foreigners Act, 1946.

According to Section 3(2)(e) of the Foreigners Act, 1946,

Central Government may by order provide that the foreigner shall comply with such conditions as may be prescribed or specified—

(i) requiring him to reside in a particular place;
(ii) imposing any restrictions on his movements;
(iii) requiring him to furnish such proof of his identity and to report such particulars to such authority in such manner and at such time and place as may be prescribed or specified...'
iv) Moreover, according to Section 3(2)(g) of the Foreigners Act, 1946, 'the Central Government may by order provide that the foreigner shall be arrested and detained or confined.'

However, India's 10 operational detention centres suffer from multiple problems ranging from infrastructure deficiency to undermining the rights of those detained. A 2018 National Human Rights Commission (NHRC) report[133] on detention centres for suspected illegal migrants in Assam, showed disturbing realities highlighting the legalities of their citizenship and the conditions of these centres. Extreme distress and suffering was reported at the two centres visited by the officials. The Goalpara detention centre (which has detainees from eight districts of Assam) and the Kokrajhar detention centre (the only women's detention centre) are housed inside jails, with no clarity on the rights of these detainees. The detainees were found to have been denied rights that even Indian prisoners get in jails. Families were separated, men and women housed in different centres, a child above six years of age is usually declared a citizen and taken away from his 'foreigner' parents with no undertaking by the state to take responsibility of the same! The report emphasized

---

[133] Report on NHRC Mission to Assam's Detention Centres, 22–24 January 2018.

that once a detainee was separated from family, he/she had no visitors, no contact with family and there is no concept of parole. Fortunately, the Supreme Court[134] has now ruled that persons who have been in detention for three years be released on bail, but given that these are poor people who do not have resources to procure documents and engage lawyers, they will hardly be able to muster two sureties of one lakh rupees or more.

According to the prison authorities, waged work was a privilege accorded to Indian prisoners and since the detainees' nationality was in question, they would sit in their cells idly.

There was no guideline for these centres and so the jail authorities applied the Assam Jail Manual. It was also found that there was no prospect for their eventual freedom due to the lack of formal agreement between countries as regards deportation. The situation in the centres for women was worse. Some would cry for hours every day, suffering from pangs of separation and loneliness. This caused them to have mental health issues with lack of medical care or rehabilitation. Special vulnerabilities of detainees and of separated children were all unaddressed. These are issues that still haunt the detainees.

Another interesting fact that came to light through this report was that in the Goalpara detention centre, there were 62 convicted foreign nationals from Bangladesh, of which only four were Hindus. It was found that all of them had completed their term of punishment and were eagerly waiting to go back. Many housed in these detention centres insist on being Indian citizens who could not produce relevant documents when asked. What happens to these people? Where do they

---

[134] Supreme Court Legal Services Committee vs Union of India, Writ Petition (Civil) 1045/2018 dated 10 May 2019.

get sent back? What is their nationality? Are they stateless? Do they become unwanted refugees in what they believe is their own country? Does religion define nationality in a secular state? Does their religion cast 'doubt' on the legitimacy of their residence in India despite years and generations?

While there are many illegal migrants in detention centres who are willing to go back to their own countries, there are many others who have suffered at the hands of their own government.

A recent news article covered by Al Jazeera[135] mentions an ordeal faced by Ali, who is working at India's largest detention centre in Goalpara district in Assam. He fears that the detention centre he is helping construct could house his own brother-in-law who failed to make it in the Assam NRC list.

A petition was filed by Harsh Mander[136] in 2018 in the Supreme Court highlighting the plight of those languishing in six detention centres of Assam based on the report. He highlighted the different categories of persons in the camp:

1. Those who accept that they are foreigners and wish to be deported to their country of origin.
2. Those who were declared foreigners in ex-parte hearings.
3. Those who are stateless since no country accepts them as their nationals.

In light of this, the Supreme Court passed an order in May 2019, directing release of all illegal migrants kept in detention centres beyond a period of three years. The authorities were

---

[135] "'How is it human?': India's largest detention centre almost ready', available at: https://www.aljazeera.com/news/2020/01/human-india-largest-detention-centre-ready-200102044649934.html. Last accessed on 10 April 2020.

[136] Supreme Court Legal Services Committee vs Union of India, Writ Petition (Civil) 1045/2018 dated 10 May 2019.

instructed under the order to take their biometric, iris and fingerprints, and photos before initiating their release for record. This case is pending and till then, the rights of the detainees remain uncertain.

Subsequent to this petition, the Government of India through the Ministry of Home Affairs drew up a 39-point 'Model Detention Centre/Holding Centre/Camp Manual' for states and Union Territories (UTs). It mentions the right of the government to deport illegal migrants under Section 3(2)(c) of the Foreigners Act, 1946, with similar powers entrusted to state governments under Article 258(1) of the Constitution of India and to the UTs under Article 239(1). It also mentions a few other provisions such as facilitating stay in cities for those in the waiting period between interview with embassy and issuance of travel documents, handing over of the foreign national to detention centre after completion of sentence, standards of human dignity inside detention camps, hygiene, electricity, water, communication and security facilities, leisure, non-separation of family members, visitation rights, special needs of detainees, transgender rights, etc.

What, however, needs to be seen is whether the manual can be followed in letter and spirit. How binding is this manual on the authorities? Will there be legislation in place to protect the rights of the detainees? Will due process be followed? What about those who have already undergone the cruelties of the detention centres? What about the future regarding which the Supreme Court has already sought information?[137]

---

[137] Abbas Lalmiya Shaikh and Rabiyakhatun Abbas Shaikh, C. C. No. 352/PW/2017.

Is Secularism under Threat?

Partition and Indian Muslims[138]

The Partition of India in 1947 left a deep scar amongst the displaced and existing populations on either side. The Independence Act of 1947 of UK Parliament ruthlessly broke up a society with stronger familial ties than any other, leaving families and lives shattered as it established two dominions, India and Pakistan.

> Be it enacted by the King's most Excellent Majesty, by and with the advice and consent of the Lords Spiritual and Temporal, and Commons, in this present Parliament assembled, and by the authority of the same, as follows:
>
> 1. As from the fifteenth day of August, nineteen hundred and forty-seven, two independent Dominions shall be set up in Dominions. India, to be known respectively as India and Pakistan.
> 2. The said Dominions are hereafter in this Act referred to as the new 'Dominions', and the said fifteenth day of August is hereafter in this Act referred to as 'the appointed day'.

---

[138] Vazira Fazila-Yacoobali Zamindar. *The Long Partition and the Making of Modern South Asia: Refugees, Boundaries, Histories,* Columbia University Press, 2010.

The territories further divided by the Indian Independence Act not only divided India on religious lines but also divided families, some of whom were forced to move out due to the growing communalism, an artful strategy of the British empire to control the territory and avoid resistance to their colonial ambitions.

1. Subject to the provisions of sub-sections (3) and (4) Territories of this section, the territories of India shall be the territories under the new the sovereignty of His Majesty which, immediately before the Dominions appointed day, were included in British India except the territories which, under sub-section (2) of this section, are to be the territories of Pakistan.
2. Subject to the provisions of sub-sections (3) and (4) of this section, the territories of Pakistan shall be—
    (a) the territories which, on the appointed day, are included in the Provinces of East Bengal and West Punjab, as constituted under the two following sections
    (b) the territories which, at the date of the passing of this Act, are included in the Province of Sind and the Chief Commissioner's Province of British Baluchistan; and
    (c) if, whether before or after the passing of this Act but before the appointed day, the Governor-General declares that the majority of the valid votes cast in the referendum which, at the date of the passing of this Act, is being or has recently been held in that behalf under his authority in

the North West Frontier Province are in favour of representatives of that Province taking part in the Constituent Assembly of Pakistan, the territories which, at the date of the passing of this Act, are included in that Province.

This partition of territories forming Indian and Pakistani soil respectively saw families stranded amidst violence, forced to choose a side to the fight not of their making. Balochistan, North West Frontier Province and provinces of East Bengal and West Punjab became territories of Pakistan hosting large numbers of both Hindu and Muslim populations. The Muslim League's demand for the formation of Pakistan since the 1930s as an Islamic state, independent of India, was myopic. Left behind as a parting gift by the British, Partition divided families, faith and peace. Independent India and Pakistan, with their governments in place, could not contain the fear of persecution in the minds of people, leading to communal hate and violence on both sides of the border creating a refugee crisis, that neither country was prepared for. South Asia experienced the largest migration of the world across the east and west border.

Muslim minorities in India, post-Partition, had no place to stay due to communal hate and violence coupled with legal barriers to their fundamental, civic and political rights, thus, evacuating Muslim residences to accommodate the huge influx of Hindu and Sikh migrants from Pakistan. Mahatma Gandhi's condition to break his fast that started on 12 January 1948 was primarily the resettlement of the Muslims back in their own houses. This condition was virtually impossible to follow due to the thousands of refugees (Hindus and

Sikhs) who were accommodated from West Pakistan in these evacuated houses.

The Indian government introduced Emergency Permit System in July 1948, which brought in two different types of permits in India largely to contain the refugee traffic: permit for Permanent Resettlement for Hindus and Sikhs, and Permit for Permanent Return for the Muhajirs. Procedurally separated on grounds of religion with a different entry requirement into the country resonates with the current regime's amendment. Permit for Permanent Return was fraught with bureaucratic hurdles that made it difficult for Muhajirs to return to India and be declared citizens. In the meantime, the evacuation of Muslim houses became legally backed by the Evacuee Property Legislation, 1950. The purpose of the legislation was to rehabilitate the Hindu and Sikh refugees who had come from West Pakistan to India. A custodian was appointed who would take charge of the houses evacuated by the Muslims in India and those Muslims were either accommodated in the 'Muslim Zones' like Purana Qila, Sadar Bazaar and Jama Masjid in Delhi or packed in trains and sent to Pakistan. It would be naïve to believe that only Hindus and Sikhs were entering India to seek refuge. Muslims residing in Pakistan pre-Partition and those who left India post-Partition were among the many who sought to return. Such was the displacement coupled with the brewing communal violence that both governments (India and Pakistan) signed the Delhi Pact, 1950, also called the Nehru–Liaquat Pact, to safeguard minority interests on both sides of the border. The objectives of the Act were stated to be as follows:

> The Governments of India and Pakistan solemnly agree that each shall ensure, to the minorities throughout its territory, complete equality of citizenship, irrespective of religion, a full sense of security in respect of life, culture, property and personal honour, freedom of movement within each country and freedom of occupation, speech and worship, subject to law and morality. Members of the minorities shall have equal opportunity with members of the majority community to participate in the public life of their country, to hold political or other office, and to serve in their country's civil and armed forces.
>
> Both Governments declare these rights to be fundamental and undertake to enforce them effectively. The Prime Minister of India has drawn attention to the fact that these rights are guaranteed to all minorities in India by its Constitution. The Prime Minister of Pakistan has pointed out that similar provision exists in the Objectives Resolution adopted by the Constituent Assembly of Pakistan. It is the policy of both Governments that the enjoyment of these democratic rights shall be assured to all their nationals without distinction. Both Governments wish to emphasise that the allegiance and loyalty of the minorities is to the State of which they are citizens, and that it is to the Government of their own State that they should look for the redress of their grievances.

The idea was to allay minority fears and create an atmosphere of peace. In the meantime, due to a large exodus of migrants, temporary permits began to be handed over to people coming from Pakistan, on the expiry of which criminal proceedings were initiated for overstaying. The promise of citizenship through the permit system saw an inherent bias against its treatment to Hindus and Sikhs vis-à-vis Muslims. Evacuee legislation was instrumental in granting permits. Due to the Delhi Pact, a large number of Muslims came on temporary permits to dispose of their properties in India before the Custodian of Evacuee was handed over command of the same. A form with questions on evacuee property became part of the permit applications. If a person was found with an allotted property in Pakistan, he was deemed an 'evacuee' in India. A new category of 'intending evacuee' was introduced to enlarge the pool of evacuees. Anyone who prepared to migrate to Pakistan became an intending evacuee whose property would now fall under the Custodian's authority. Another interesting legislation passed was the Evacuee Interest Separation Act, 1951, affecting joint family properties. The burden of proof lay on the Muslims to establish that they were not evacuees or that they had not gone or did not have any future intention of migrating to Pakistan. A long process of proving 'no intention to migrate' to Pakistan was through show of ration cards, municipal records and other documents embroiling Indian Muslims in an exhausting process of establishing their national identity—an NRC-like situation post-Partition. All of these indicated that permits challenged citizenship and deported those found guilty of violating their permits while evacuee could dispossess thousands despite them being citizens. The Government of India abrogated the Evacuee law in 1954 as realization struck that Muslims were being dispossessed. The Permit System was replaced with the Passport System in 1967.

Partition and subsequent legislations separated families forever. Travelling across border to meet with relatives could signify intent to migrate while journeys of adventure across border for rebellious youths could also mean loss of nationality through application of the same principle.

Shah Mohammad[139] was one such case of youthful exuberance that resulted in loss of citizenship. Shah went to Pakistan for a trip with his friends at the age of 15 without the knowledge and consent of his father, who had opted to stay and work in India. His family argued on his behalf that there was no intention on Shah's part to migrate to Pakistan. He was stranded in Pakistan, waiting to come back to his own country. He acquired a Pakistani passport as a last resort and came back to India applying for the Permit for Permanent Return which was refused. The lower court and the Allahabad High Court ruled in his favour on the grounds that he was a minor and his departure could not be construed as intent to permanently settle in Pakistan. However, the Supreme Court in 1969, overruled the High Court's judgement, relinquishing all powers of determining citizenship to the Union Government.

Another peculiar case was that of Hidayathunissa Begum,[140] whose husband migrated to Pakistan and acquired Pakistani citizenship while she remained in India. She and her children applied for an Indo-Pak passport[141] in 1958 to visit her husband, but the authorities questioned their nationality in the first place. According to the law, her stay in India was unauthorized since her husband had acquired Pakistani nationality and by virtue

---

[139] Vazira Fazila-Yacoobali Zamindar. *The Long Partition and the Making of Modern South Asia: Refugees, Boundaries, Histories*-Columbia University Press, 2010, p. 215.

[140] ibid. p. 212.

[141] A special system designed for travel between India and Pakistan only until the Passport Act came into effect.

of patrilocal residence, she was a Pakistani herself. And thus, they became Pakistani citizens despite never having been to Pakistan.

In Taskin Ahmad's case,[142] it was noted by authorities that he was a Pakistani national who had come to India on a visa in 1955. After having visited his family and native village in Uttar Pradesh, he went back to Pakistan, making a second visit in 1957. It was found that he had supposedly crossed the border and stayed back in India until his arrest in 1974. During that period, he got married and had six children. At his trial, he was able to show his birth certificate which indicated him to be an Indian citizen by birth (born in Kanpur). He showed other documents such as electoral list, village register, etc., with his name in them. However, he could not produce any documentary proof showing his presence in India on 26 January 1950. A natural interpretation of the Citizenship Act, 1955, and its Rules was that once a person acquires a foreign passport, he loses Indian citizenship. In addition to this, as we understand from Shah Mohammad's case, the question of citizenship was determined by the Central Government which was pending in his case for years. The Delhi High Court had quashed his conviction but had not acquitted him. It is rather unfortunate a case and there are many others. For a man who was born in India, lived most part of his life in India except a few years (1955 and 1957), had a family in India among other things, going to Pakistan after serving his sentence in India would not have guaranteed being recognized a citizen in Pakistan. Does this form of statelessness orchestrated by

---

[142] Salman Khurshid, *At Home in India: The Muslim Saga*. Hay House India, 2014

bureaucratic hurdles serve any justice?

Questions are posed on one's nationality on the basis of religion. Muslims, even today, are viewed as naturally disloyal to the nation in popular perception. The M.S. Satyu film *Garam Hava* brilliantly portrays the fate of ordinary Indian Muslims after Partition. In more recent times, the film *Bombay* takes the story forward to the grim reality of their existence many decades later. Yet, the last word on Partition seems to have been said by the film *Jinnah* made by a Pakistani team. As Jinnah, played by Christopher Lee, after his demise, reports to the divine record-keeper played by Shashi Kapoor, it is discovered that his computer data is missing. He is, therefore, asked to rapidly live his life as though in fast-track to recover the record. Having done that to the record-keeper's satisfaction (and obviously having had a chance to reflect upon his life), he requests one short visit to complete something important. On being permitted, he travels to the newly carved border between India and Pakistan, where cartloads of migrants are crossing each other. He goes up to one packed cart and noticing a small child asks her where she was going. The girl responded, 'I am going to Pakistan to ask Mr Jinnah what he had done to my mother.' The girl's father, recognizing Jinnah, rushes to apologize on her behalf explaining that she did not know who he was. Jinnah waves him aside and speaks to the child, 'You are a brave girl. Pakistan was made so that you are safe. But I hope I will be forgiven for my part in this.'

As we read the history of the times, it becomes more and more apparent how ordinary mistakes of important people lead to unprecedented developments causing untold misery and pain to ordinary people. Also, that history is not quite as inevitable as we might think, much later having gotten used to it. But of course this is no time to review or reimagine history except to guard against attempts to twist and distort it to demonize the hapless victims, the community of Indian Muslims who chose to remain where they belonged, repudiating the two-nation theory and sacrificing bonds of family and friendship.

The most fervent appeals to Muslims not to depart came from Maulana Abul Kalam Azad and the much younger Dr Zakir Husain, both true nationalists and devoted to Mahatma Gandhi. But the promise and reassurances, they and other national leaders like Jawaharlal Nehru made, were to be put through severe test in times to come. Periodic communal violence followed the tone set by Partition; violence rising to a gory crescendo in north India in the 1980s, the Mumbai riots, in 1992-93 and finally, Gujarat in 2002. (The anti-Sikh riots though unrelated to the legacy of Partition, only added to the dismal landscape.) The most recent flare ups in northeast Delhi after the CAA protests come as a reminder that urban communal violence may not yet be an embarrassing past of a rapidly modernizing India.

Communal violence happened periodically, but the remarkable resilience of the people (presumably victims and perpetrators alike) quickly papered the cracks if not repaired them entirely. But meanwhile, something was happening—or rather not happening—in our society that cast a shadow on the promise of 1947. Despite conspicuous achievements such as electing three Muslim presidents, elevating four Chief Justice of India, appointing a chief of the Air Force, a cabinet secretary, foreign minister, chief election commissioner, director of IB, et al. who were Muslims, the community continued to suffer participation imbalances. This was highlighted by the Sachar Committee and the Justice Ranganath Mishra Commission. But for a variety of reasons, the ambitious affirmative action programme remained in a slow start mode. Then the public mood changed, distorting notions of justice into a charge of appeasement for votes. Ultimately, nothing was left but wild charges of anti-nationalism that mock the supreme sacrifice of noble men such as Brigadier Usman and Havildar Abdul Hamid and the galaxy of freedom fighters.

Why the Debate about Dissent?

In a recent lecture, Justice Deepak Gupta[143] underscored that 'Criticism of the executive, the judiciary, the bureaucracy and the armed forces cannot be termed sedition,' and that:

> If we stifle criticism of these institutions, we shall become a police state instead of a democracy... For me, there is a very important right which is not spelt out in the Constitution...the right of freedom of opinion, the right of freedom of conscience, by themselves, include the most important right: the right to dissent... New thinkers are born when they disagree with well-accepted norms of the society... If everybody follows the well-trodden path, no new path will be created and no new vistas of the mind will be found.

The Judge then drove the point home thus:

> The destruction of spaces for questioning and dissent destroys the basis of all growth—political, economic, cultural and social. In this sense, dissent is a safety valve of democracy. The blanket labelling of dissent as anti-

---

[143] Available at: https://www.livelaw.in/videos/democracy-and-dissent-powerful-speech-by-justice-deepak-gupta-154166. Last accessed on 3 April 2020.

national or anti-democratic strikes at the heart of our commitment to protect constitutional values and the promotion of deliberative democracy.

In a similar vein, Justice D.Y. Chandrachud at another lecture said that protecting dissent is but a reminder that a democratically elected government can never claim a 'monopoly over the values and identities' that define the country's plural society. The attack on dissent strikes at the heart of a dialogue-based democratic society and hence, a state is required to ensure that it deploys its machinery to protect the freedom of speech and expression within the bounds of law, and dismantle any attempt to instil fear or curb free speech.[144]

Chief Justice A.P. Shah (retired) went even further in a memorial lecture. Speaking of several distressing dimensions of contemporary national life, he said,

> In the midst of all of this, there is a positive, heartening moment like the protests we are seeing today, against the Citizenship Amendment Act, and everything that it stands for. When students—from all over the country, including from institutions like Jawaharlal Nehru University, Jamia Millia, Aligarh Muslim University, St Stephens, who collectively embody the future of a nation—come together in a peaceful protest against an unjust and unconstitutional law, it is an act that citizens of any democracy should be proud of.[145]

---

[144] Available at: https://www.youtube.com/watch?v=JeSCUEDPoiQ. Last accessed on 3 April 2020.
[145] Available at: https://scroll.in/article/952775/justice-ap-shah-freedoms-on-unsteady-ground-made-to-doubt-whether-sc-able-to-protect-our-rights. Last accessed on 3 April 2020.

Yet, innumerable young person continue to live in constant fear of the midnight knock; their lofty, noble commitment to constitutional democracy put in the dock of criminality. This is a generation that chose the democratic path even as tales of desperation and hopelessness were attempting to push their contemporaries to reject democracy. We owe a debt to them in more ways than one, and these valuable assets must not be treated in a manner that leaves permanent scars on their personality or careers.

Public Response to CAA–NRC–NPR and Civil Disobedience

Disobedience in a democracy[146] has suddenly become central to our public discourse in recent times because of the protests inspired by Shaheen Bagh which, in turn, was a reaction to police entering the Jamia University campus on 15 December 2019 and assaulting students in the Dr Zakir Husain Library. Clearly, the government has no idea about the concept of civil disobedience, but there is some reason to believe that people opposed to the government's position might also be mistaken about its dimensions.

Several state assemblies have passed resolutions opposing the CAA–NRC–NPR and state chief ministers have made statements about their determination not to implement NRC–NPR. Yet, direct questions about the impact of the resolutions on Parliamentary legislation, answered honestly, caused great discomfiture amongst activists. Wisdom has it that you ask a stupid question, you get a stupid answer. Instead, self-opinionated experts should have focussed on the concept

---

[146] Peter Singer, *Democracy and Disobedience*. Clarendon Press, 1973.

of democratic disobedience to buttress moral resistance to an unjust law. There may well be a difference between the disobedience by a citizen and that of a constitutional authority like the state assembly. Understandably, there are greater constraints on the latter. Yet, it is arguable that federalism has its own scope for disobedience beyond the restricted technical textual dimensions. As the notion of constitutional morality is seen in current jurisprudence as an overarching presence, federalism too must be seen as a touchstone for the constitutional balance between the Centre and the states. Federalism as an idea beyond the text of the constitutional provisions needs to be given a serious look.

Disobedience to law in a democracy and its justification depends a great deal on the quality of democracy we have. A law passed by the duly elected members of Parliament must ordinarily be obeyed, particularly by those who hold office by virtue of law and the Constitution. Then, of course, there is the Supreme Court, which has the last word on the validity of the law. Symbolic disobedience may be justified at any stage even to make a point in Parliament and the courts. But protesting a law that has the approval of the courts is a little more difficult to justify. Of course, there is the fact that the Supreme Court is neither infallible nor claims to be so. It has been known to change its view of the law, sometimes within a short time. But so long as a judgement holds, it has to be respected, if nothing, to preserve the standing of the court, which itself is crucial to our governance.

There are other issues to keep in mind as well. Gandhian Satyagraha or civil disobedience is essentially a moral assertion and relies on examples to make a point. A person who chose to take part in civil disobedience is prepared to suffer the sanction for breaking the law. Therefore, he/she makes it a point to suffer and not seek forgiveness or mitigation of the consequence (punishment). But it is of course another matter that their defiance of law causes unintended discomfort or inconvenience to others, both sympathizers as well as those who are neutral. But then others cannot be too demanding and place their rights entirely above those of the protesters as conscientious objectors. Finding the balance is the ultimate test of democracy.

The road that civil disobedience takes is not an easy or a short one. Before stepping out, one has to be ready for a long-distance journey; any expectation of rapid response and relief might well be lethal to the endeavour, particularly if one is against insensitive and conceited establishment. Hope is an important ingredient of civil disobedience, holding the individuals back from crossing over to revolt and rebellion. Despite the anguish and frustration, the individual does not reject the system in entirety. The movement identified with Jamia University and Shaheen Bagh is wonderfully connected with the Constitution and national symbols, truly inclusive and participatory. There is no scope for failure because that would be defeat of the Constitution and all that it means to the citizen. Unfortunately, the attempts by police authorities to paint all young activists with anti-national hues will cause irreparable damage to democracy.

Once the battle for basic equality and dignity is won, there will be many other fields to conquer. We cannot rest drawing the line of resistance at equal citizenship because all the issues due to which this drastic step was initiated must be addressed: harmony between faiths, equal opportunity for all—education, healthcare, housing and gainful employment—

and not as handouts for popularity but for the empowerment of each citizen in our lifetime. A liberal democracy, according to the political philosopher John Rawls, ensures that people have maximum liberty consistent with equal liberty for others. Furthermore, any difference between people is permissible if it is to the maximum advantage of the disadvantaged. Our pervasive pragmatism generally overwhelms this principle of justice. We have a chance, indeed an imperative, to subscribe to a fresh compact with the people to meticulously implement those principles. We need not worry about the cynics who cry wolf at the slightest sound because our Constitution provides ample safeguards of reasonable restrictions in order to protect the edifice of liberty from inimical forces. But those safeguards have to be applied with the greatest sense of responsibility, in the spirit of a sacred trust. Human dignity can be undermined in many ways: illegitimate incarceration, state brutality, economic assault, mass media defamation, etc. Every human being deserves equal concern and respect, particularly when we disagree with their views. The right to disagree is a pivotal moral right.

People have different impressions about the CAA–NRC–NPR protests happening across India. Some are impressed, others curious whilst a few are puzzled. As much as Amit Shah would have us to believe that there is no evidence of large-scale public support for CAA, it is undeniable that the trigger may have been the spontaneous reaction in Muslim-dominated areas and institutions. However, from the beginning, citizens of different faiths have participated in the protests with determination and conviction. It was truly an inclusive endeavour untouched by party political ambition. Shaheen Bagh voted for the AAP but silently and without celebration or any expectation of quid pro quo. There is no clear leadership structure beyond a degree of consensual management. A close observation of the composition of participants discloses a wide range, from conservative Right to outspoken Left with a mixture of broad liberals. All were unequivocally committed to the cause but periodically suffer relapse of ideological stubbornness. This can cause irreversible damage to the movement if allowed to prevail upon collective pragmatism. One cannot assume that every step a government takes is unwarranted and wrong; or the Opposition's view is by definition always correct. It is another matter that having been in government one might review one's position in the Opposition with the advantage of hindsight. What else explains the attitude of the master of disruption, Arvind Kejriwal, to Shaheen Bagh? But hopefully, all politics is not about electoral profit and loss account.

Understandably, even before dismantling the protest site because of COVID-19, the longevity of the protests was a looming concern amongst the participants and their well-wishers. The cause raised is so critical for constitutional governance that its failure will cause irreversible damage to our democracy. Thus far, the arm's length support of political parties has been politically correct, but given the obdurate and insensitive attitude of the government, it is a moot question if the movement can be sustained in its present form. The choice then, of the timing of transformation of the present pan-India movement into a full-scale political campaign if so decided by the protagonists, must be made by them. On the other hand, political parties may choose to draw a longer line and gradually subsume the cause with the present participants aligning with their preferred political parties. The months to come will surely see important developments.

Having underscored the inclusive nature of the protests and constant efforts to defame and defile the protesters, it is important to put the record straight on their objective. No protester has ever questioned the decision to grant citizenship to Hindus and Sikhs who had stayed on in Pakistan after Partition but decided to move to India at a later date once citizenship laws were put in place and passports introduced for travellers. Indeed, they wonder why this concern is being limited to 2014 and not being shown to those who need the indulgence after the cut-off date. This could have been done easily under the unamended Citizenship Act, 1955, read with the Citizenship Rules, 1956, and the present amendment was therefore quite unnecessary. People cannot be blamed for reading motives. The problem is that the candidates for citizenship are to be identified by their religion and a virtual presumption of persecution. On the other hand, persons actually subjected to persecution such as the Ahmadiyyas and Baloch of Pakistan, Tamils of Sri Lanka, et al. are excluded along with all persons persecuted for political views or social mores. The government has been at pains to prove that no Indian citizen need to worry about CAA and in any case, that it is about granting citizenship and not taking it away. The government is obviously unable to decipher tautologies. Indian citizens need not worry; but those who are unable to establish their citizenship have a great deal to worry.

The real sting is in NRC–NPR, and CAA is but the balm for some who might be singed by the former. But even the arguably intended beneficiaries will be at a loss to establish their Pakistan, Bangladesh or Afghanistan citizenship having failed to establish their Indian citizenship. Be that as it may, the protests were not only about the relief balm being proposed selectively and that too, on religious grounds—that will cause discrimination to the protesters themselves but their assertion as citizens that discrimination must not happen at all. All Indian citizens have a right to insist that their government honours the constitutional principles they hold sacrosanct. This protest was not so much about the likely impact on individual interests as it is about implications for our constitutional governance. Once the constitutional integrity of our polity is breached, there is no telling how far we will slide.

There is another important dimension of these protests: the convergence of private with public. Unlike most protests where men choose to leave their womenfolk safely at home, these protests were being led by women and young girls. Entire families participate, particularly at the sit-ins, round the clock. Arrangements were made for food and rest. Since children too come in large numbers and participate actively, there were arrangements to teach them as well. Their knowledge and awareness were a delight to watch, like a virtual replay of the child at the barricades in *Les Misérables*. With these angels of democracy, it is mean to doubt their complete commitment to the Constitution. In doubting slogans of 'azaadi', their detractors are only showing disrespect to the Constitution, from where they claim liberty. It is only willing pathological slaves who do not understand the nobility of Justice, Equality, Liberty and Fraternity mentioned in the Preamble to the Constitution.

Sadly, some media anchors and other persons repeatedly complain about the use of the word 'azaadi' by protesters against CAA–NRC–NPR. They pretend or stupidly believe it has something to do with secession and betrayal of India, a false narrative created by the media against student activists of

JNU. Self-opinionated judgemental condemnation follows as they play the accuser, prosecutor, judge and jury. One of them glibly said to me that this is what an average Indian believes and liberals walk into a trap each time they support any such claim of azaadi. Let us therefore look closer at the slogans that are generally chanted to boost the morale of the protesters:

> *Hum kya chahte: Azaadi*
> *Hum le ke raheinge: Azaadi*
> *Hum cheen ke lainge: Azaadi*
> *Jaan se pyari: Azaadi*
> *Pyari pyari: Azadi*
> *Azaad desh mein: Azaadi*
> *Tum kuch bhi karlo: Azaadi*
> *Tum jail mein dalo: Azaadi*
> *Tum goli maro: Azaadi*
> *Chua choot se: Azaadi*
> *Bhukmari se: Azaadi*
> *Berozgari se: Azaadi*
> *Gandhi jaisi: Azaadi*
> *Ashfaq jaisi: Azaadi*
> *Awaaz na aai: Azaadi*
> *Azaad desh mein: Azaadi*
> *Jamia ki larkiyon ne rasta dikhaya hai: Jamia ki larkiyon ko inqalab, zindabad*
> *Zulmi jab jab zulm karenga satta ke galiyaron se: Chappa chappa goonj uthega inqalab ke naron se*
> *Kya dar gaya, kya mar gaya, muthee taan ke uncha bol: Halla bol, halla bol*
> *Awaaz na aayee zor se bol: Halla bol, halla bol*

Awaaz do: Hum ek hain
Hindustan: Zindabad
Samvidhan: Zindabad
Larenge: Jeetenge
Abhi se kya batayen kya hamare dil mein hai: Waqt aane par batadenge tujhe ai aasman
Safaroshi ki tamanna ab hamare dil mein hai: Dekhna hai zor kitna baazu-e-qatil mein hai
Bol re saathi halla bol: Halla bol, halla bol
Communal violence pe uncha bol: Halla bol, halla bol
Inqlabo, inqalabo, inqalabo, inqalab: Zindabad, zindabad, zindabad, zindabad.

Thus, it is all about azaadi and inquilab (revolution). In the history of human endeavour, those two wonderful words might not have been more reviled and abused, even by despots and their storm troopers, than by BJP supportive media and troll guerrillas. If words can be treated as violence, this is no less than a daily blood bath without remorse. The tragic thing is that the protagonists self-righteously believe their view of azaadi is infallible and entitles them to ridicule and humiliate their opponents. This lot is unnerved by the resilience of Shaheen Bagh and having done their utmost to defame and demoralize the ladies at the barricades, they resorted to a refrain for terminating the protest as though the nation's future depends on it. Perhaps, they are, at least ironically, right in saying that dismantling of the protest might well be the undermining of democracy.

But to get back to the allergy to azaadi: why do we need to seek azaadi after 1947? We are asked with glib fake patriotism, disguising crass and petty ambition. Well, how about reading the Preamble to the Constitution? Does it not mention Justice, Liberty, Equality and Fraternity? Does Liberty not translate as azaadi? Does the press not cherish and demand 'Freedom of Expression'? Does Article 19 of the Constitution not guarantee freedom of movement, assembly, residence, association, profession? Has the court not recently said that Section 144 of the CrPC cannot be used to deny those freedoms?

When the women of Shaheen Bagh seek to enforce their rights under the Constitution, those who purport to question that are undermining that very Constitution. There cannot be a greater betrayal of the commitment of every Indian to that noble document. When the government supports such constitutional delinquents, it violates its solemn oath of office. What makes it sad is their cynical belief that this will divide the nation to their political advantage. That, only time will tell. For the present, we can draw satisfaction—if not joy—from the fact that the women of Shaheen Bagh have made the Constitution a part of enlightened discourse and the tricolour a constant companion in our tryst with freedom. Their determination and resolve have challenged what the incumbent government had believed was their invincibility. Switching from ridicule to forced disruption and unwarranted arrests is an obvious admission of their vulnerability and intellectual bankruptcy.

If dramatic results beyond one's imagination had not become the order of the day, the latest stunning statistics of the 2020 Delhi assembly elections might have allowed a comment or two. But honestly, what does one say about a national party getting zero seats in the state that it gloriously ruled for 15 years and which gave late Sheila Dikshit a permanent place in history? Besides, attempting to react with honesty triggers unexpected reactions from friends and foes alike, followed on the heels by the media that seems to relish the Congress party eating humble pie. The defeat (mild as that word might sound) includes the tumbling of several leaders of considerable experience and weight just as AAP's sweep includes any number of lightweights. But then the winner, particularly who takes all, is not to be dismissed easily.

Of course as a national party that held sway in Delhi for 15 years, the Congress party needs to know why it lost, and that too badly, if it is to show continued relevance to the national discourse. Curiously, many of the dedicated and determined CAA-NRC protesters who undoubtedly silently voted for the AAP (even though they had doubts about its position) appeared strangely subdued the night of the victory of their chosen candidates. They seemed not to have found a way out or forward in the moment of electoral success but focussed on their own endeavours as though nothing had changed. Their concerns are obviously much larger than an election, though there must be a sense of relief that the proverbial electric current (read: shock) of Amit Shah stung him rather than the fatigued army of constitutional peace warriors at Jamia University and Shaheen Bagh.

The protesters must be wondering what to do next as indeed the newly elected AAP government too must be trying to figure it out. For the present, the horrific intervention of COVID-19 has suspended the democratic possibilities. There is also the matters pending in the Supreme Court about the constitutional validity of CAA; the continuing protests that have blocked roads for two months and counting; the concern expressed by the Chief Justice about little infants accompanying their parents to the protest sites (triggered by a letter written to the court by a student from Mumbai after the unfortunate death of a four-month-old child). These protests are *sue generis* indeed in their spontaneity and conspicuous absence of organized leadership as indeed being devoid of any overt or covert political party support. But they are also interestingly and overwhelmingly populated by women, not just emancipated activist class but also the run-of-the-mill middle-class conservatives. Participants come as family units with the children being up front in enthusiasm and involvement. They can be sympathetically persuaded and counselled, but it might be very difficult to give them directions. To deal with this unique breed of protesters, we need to understand the philosophy behind civil disobedience and Satyagraha instead of relying upon stale techniques of law and order. The court might have to play the parent, teacher, counsellor, manager and leader rolled into one to be able to reach the hearts and minds of these people.

One can understand that the Central Government has rigid faith in its decision and despite the Delhi election result, it might not be persuaded to rethink its position. However, if Amit Shah's statements are anything to go by, there is no reason to complain because CAA is not anti-Muslim or against minorities in general. There are two problems with his articulation: first, that the crowds gathering are entirely Muslim; and second, that people can complain only if they are actually affected and not if they merely disagree with the government in its effort to convert religion-neutral concept of citizenship into a religion-conscious exercise. Every Indian surely has a right to demand that the policies of the State do not violate the constitutional commitment of equality. Departure from that, even if it does not directly affect any citizen today, may well open the gates to more harmful discrimination in the future. Shaheen Bagh is not by Muslims, for Muslims, of Muslims. It is about Indians and Muslims too are Indians.

As these questions loom over the political horizon, the Congress party has to dig the barren soil to prepare it for planting fresh seeds. It may not have the benefit of the concession that it need not look for answers to the problem so long as it register its moral support and stand by protesters who are roughed up by State agencies. The form of institutional civil disobedience such as State Assembly Resolutions to oppose CAA-NRC-NPR will obviously have to move from symbolism to substantive defiance. But meanwhile, the party has to get back to the drawing board even as it rediscovers its roots. It is time to realize that the politics of freebies is not sustainable and ultimately, the politics of freedom will and must prevail. But people have to experience loss of freedom before they learn its value. We are being drawn into the former and must strive for the latter, or as Janis Joplin sang:

> *Freedom's just another word for nothing left to lose*
> *And nothing isn't worth nothing if it ain't free*
> *Feeling good was easy, Lord, when Bobby sang the blues*
> *And buddy, feeling good was good enough for me*
> *Good enough for me and my Bobby McGee.*

Shaheen Bagh and Jamia protesters have become role models for thousands of protest sites across the country. Never before has the theme of patriotism been expressed and highlighted in protests with such intensity. Most protests are about felt democratic deficits and ultimately find a level of accommodation between the protesters and the establishment. Shaheen Bagh et al. are about honouring the heart and soul of the Constitution or what the Supreme Court describes as constitutional morality. It is still early days to be able to predict the trajectory this movement will take. Decision-making amongst the protagonists remains somewhat amorphous and unstructured; no clear leadership has emerged and loosely collective decisions continue to sustain the effort. Some voluntary assistance in kind shores up the contribution of organizers. People await timeline events such as Supreme Court and High Court hearing dates in the hope that their narrative will move forward. Yet, the protests have become a daily routine poised in a delicate balance between here and now on one hand and constant rumours about impending action to evict them and put an end to their democratic protests. A feeler was given at Khureji where a peaceful protest that had been going on for 50 days was ruthlessly dispersed and the stage and equipment dismantled. It was surprising that this happened despite repeated pronouncements of appellate courts that people have a right to protest and disagreement with government cannot be termed anti-national. The young and feisty lawyer, Ishrat Jahan, bravely led the movement from the front till she was unfairly arrested.

It is important that this democratic impulse is not allowed to fizzle out. Although it is more than clear that the movement is neither exclusive nor self-centred around minority concerns and instead is wonderfully inclusive, its distractors continue to situate it in communal space. The members of majority community as indeed other minorities who have joined the movement whole-heartedly and the resonance of national sentiment along with public display of constitutional allegiance make this protest unique in its plurality even if the initial upsurge came from Muslims. No longer self-conscious or silenced by political correctness, Muslims have claimed their equal political space without the slightest hint of being anyone's vote bank. It is an Indian protest through and through at a time when claim to Indianness (Bhartiyata) has been sought to be a monopoly of an abrasive section. For long have those people demanded proof of nationalist commitment as though they have a right to seek it. Now that national symbols are made the stock and trade of popular patriotism and religious pronouncements relegated to personal life without effacing cultural attributes, the self-opinionated, self-appointed defenders of constitutional faith are left perplexed. Having lost the battle of big ideas, they have scurried to scream about public inconvenience and obstruction of public spaces. These very people saw no wrong in religious fervour obstructing streets for days on end or lethal attacks on innocent people using public utilities for normal purposes. All rights must indeed accommodate other people's rights, but the balance must be an objective one. The genesis of Shaheen Bagh is in a sense that the scales have not of late been even and therefore caused a concern about impending public policy decisions or their implementation. It is, therefore, not enough to expect Shaheen Bagh protesters to show courtesies and accommodation but important to give them a feeling that their views matter. Furthermore, their views need not be restricted to their own prospects and future but include what they believe is good and right for the country. Their opinion must matter as that of any other person.

One wonders if the mediators appointed by the Supreme Court who reached out to Shaheen Bagh protesters talked about traffic facilitation or the cause of the protest too. If no one talks to them about the merits of their complaints, there may be a good reason for obstruction, but not if there is a substantive dialogue, albeit unsuccessful. Shaheen Bagh must not be reduced to an inconvenience because the reach, in this case, will be watched by hundreds of other similar protests across the country, even though most of them may not pose physical problems akin to the former. The Supreme Court should be concerned with how dissent and disagreement are treated in our polity rather than limit its concern to traffic regulation. That it might do by indicating the need for the government to show some accommodation even without compromising its ideology and ultimately showing signals of its intent to quickly examine the constitutional validity of CAA and the bearing it has on NRC. Recent judgements of the court and some extrajudicial pronouncements of certain top judges show a strong trend of rights-oriented decisions. Yet, there are several important questions relating to the liberty of the citizen that are to be decided and many people feel that greater urgency might have been shown in dealing with them. Article 370 of the Constitution and CAA are two important issues pending in the court although the curbing of the Internet in Jammu and Kashmir has been expeditiously decided with somewhat varied results based on the ground reality. Similarly, imposition of the Public Safety Act (PSA) on senior leaders of Jammu and Kashmir remains to be tested. Shaheen Bagh has discovered its voice of liberty, there is no reason to confine it to one dimension of democratic rights. Hopefully, the followers of the 'Idea of India' will be encouraged by this voice to converge in a nationwide movement for rediscovery of freedom, confining to the dustbin of history myths about minorities, women and most of all, about the majority community.

It is imperative that the national discourse is brought back to reason and civility. The nature and content of the CAA protest will have a great contribution to make. The opposite side, whose provocative and hate-filled statements were the prelude to heartless rioting in northeast Delhi, needs to be disabused about their capacity to hurt Indian unity. This too is the task that the legacy of these protests will achieve. These are thus not protests, but an affirmation of hope. But sadly, the Delhi police, whose several decisions remain under a cloud and subject to court proceedings, have chosen to ascribe the worst character to the protest. And this too when they should be dealing with blatant and devious efforts by a large section of the electronic media to project the indiscretions of the Tablighi Jamaat[147] as virtual bio-war against the Indian state. Surviving COVID-19 calls for unity of purpose and trust, not myopia or giving communal colour. We will survive the pandemic, as we must, but if in the process we lose our moorings as a liberal society, it will be a tragic chapter in the history of India.

---

[147] Three-day congregation at the Markaz on 13–15 March 2020, though before lockdown but after vigilant people had started social distancing.

Annexure

Letter to Freedom's Child:
Mahira Sayyed, born on 29 May 2016

Dearest Child of Freedom,

I see you at the barricades, daily equipped with nothing but your belief in the Constitution. You sport a badge on your tiny chest proclaiming allegiance to the Constitution. I am not certain if you have even read the noble document or are old enough to know its text. But you trust it as you do your own family, your parents in whose arms you position yourself and lead many grown-up with slogans spanning your name—freedom to the revolution. You know not fear or doubt. 'Put us in prison: we will seek azaadi.' Curious that you are seeking what you are, freedom. To begin with I felt an outsider as though the fight was someone else's and I was a sympathizer. You ran into my arms and called me dada and instantly made me feel wanted. The fight was yours and mine besides all others who had gathered as well as those who cannot be there.

With all the courage and self-confidence that your voice and demeanour display, what is most interesting is the unqualified hope that you possess. Sadly, life's experience may have dented some of the hope that we had, or even the determination to take on life's challenges we once had. Yet, the battering that life gives vanishes with a look at your smile and your voice ringing in my years. They say when a child is born, she can see God and therefore she smiles seemingly inexplicably. It is with passing years that God recedes, expecting humans to put in effort to search for His divinity. But you surely can still feel and see God close by and get His blessings every passing moment, even at the barricades. If you speak to God, please tell him how much I wish that he gives me strength to preserve the hope with which you come to the barricades, and indeed the hope you give to us.

Looking at you, freedom, I wonder how unlucky and deprived those people must be who have not seen you or met you. It is you who make the difference between ordinary animal existence and a human life to cherish. Generations of valiant soldiers devoted themselves to India's Independence inspired by you and long before you were born in our midst. There is much we owe you and even more to receive from you yet.

There is a promise that we must make to you: we will never let you down so long as your voice eggs us on to our destiny. We will not rest till we can be certain that all our countrymen and women, all children enjoy equal concern and respect of the government; all the rights and entitlements granted and recognized in the Constitution are actually secured to all citizens; hate has no place in society and love pervades our collective existence; fear and anger are obliterated; compassion and mercy are the hallmarks of Indians; just deserts prevail over all considerations except affirmative action; there are none lonely in the crowd; religion is a balm and a bond, not a divisive instrument; where faith is critical to our lives but neutral for the State.

I hope you will not be overwhelmed by the long list of aspirations that you have triggered. In time, you will handle all these, but right now your strength is your spirit and the hope of innocence. Right now is your age to play and have a little fun but you choose big challenges. It would be selfish of us to take that away from you only because we need your help in the struggle. But thanks for being there with us at the barricades. You have added joy to the struggle. You have made us understand that some struggles are worth joining because losing is not an option. For you, I can at this moment, do no better than to recall the words of Gurudev Rabindranath Tagore (into that Heaven of Freedom) and Allama Iqbal ('Lab pe aati hai dua'). Bless you child for growing up happy. For me, these moments of your childhood will remain a permanent talisman. When you grow up and read this, you will know the difference you made to someone's life.

With affection and prayers,

Your dada
(Salman Khurshid)

Index

42nd Amendment to the Constitution (India), 70

Aadhaar number, 18
Aam Aadmi Party (AAP), 83
Advani, L.K., 102, 103
Afghanistan, 7, 19, 21, 32, 65, 69, 70, 74, 110, 113, 117, 118, 119, 122, 123, 125, 127, 175
Ahmadiyyas, 68, 125, 126, 175
Aligarh Muslim University (AMU), 85
All Assam Gana Sangram Parishad, 132
All Assam Students' Union, 26
Ambedkar, B.R., 47, 93
anti-CAA, 23, 75, 83, 86, 87
anti-Hindu, 76, 77, 78, 80, 81
Apex Court, 24, 31, 38, 40, 44, 60, 61, 63, 65, 69
Article 5, 47, 51, 52, 111, 112
Article 14, 4, 22, 48, 61, 62, 63, 64, 65, 66, 67, 69, 121, 130, 143
Article 355, 31, 143
Assam accord, 98
Assam Movement, 131, 132
Assam Sanmilita Mahasangha, 25, 29, 44, 139, 143
Assam Sanmilita Mahasangha & Ors vs Union of India, 29

autonomous districts, 144
azaadi, 86, 176, 177, 178, 179, 187

Baloch (tribe), 117
Banerjee, Mamata, 33, 102
Bangladesh, 7, 19, 21, 25, 26, 28, 29, 31, 32, 41, 65, 70, 74, 89, 95, 97, 98, 99, 100, 101, 103, 113, 117–119, 122, 123, 125, 128, 132, 134, 139, 140, 152, 154, 175
Bangladeshi infiltrators, 29, 30, 33
Bharatiya Janata Party (BJP), 4, 80
Bhutan, 113, 126, 127, 128
blocking roads, 85
Brahuis, 124
Buddhist, 6, 21, 123, 126, 144

Census Act, 1948, 10
Christian, 6, 21, 123, 126, 144
Citizenship Act, 1955, 6, 11, 37, 48, 50, 112, 133, 134, 138, 139, 143, 146, 164, 175
Citizenship Act, 2003, 50
Citizenship Amendment Act (CAA), 21, 22, 28, 55, 90, 91, 98, 99, 102, 169
Citizenship Amendment Bill (CAB), 123
Citizenship Rules, 1956, (amendment to), 103, 175

Citizenship Rules, 2003, 16, 17, 22, 23, 24, 25, 37, 48, 50
Communist Party of India (Marxist) [CPI (M)], 97
Congress party, 16, 28, 44, 70, 97, 99, 102, 103, 180, 182
Constituent Assembly, 47, 53, 55, 56, 57, 58, 159, 161
Constitution of India, 4, 22, 31, 51, 52, 57, 58, 59, 60, 61, 69, 70, 71, 72, 88, 104, 111, 113, 156
Covid-19, 84

Dalits, 72, 77, 113
driver's licence number, 18

electoral photo identity card (EPIC), 150
Emergency Permit System of 1948, 111
Evacuee Interest Separation Act, 1951, 162

Foreigners Act, 1946, 7, 39, 40, 125, 132, 134, 138, 152, 153, 156
freedom of speech and expression, 85, 169
fundamental rights, 60, 61, 92

Gandhi, Mahatma, 60, 61, 72, 91, 92, 114, 116, 159, 166
Gehlot, Ashok, 102, 103, 117
Gogoi, Tarun, 99

Hindu Bengali refugees, 101, 102
Hindu fundamentalism, 89
Hindu Rashtra, 73, 74
Hindu refugees, 91, 99, 103
Hindutva, 4, 74, 89
Human Rights, 115, 124, 130, 153
Husain, Dr Zakir, 116, 166, 170

illegal migrants, 20, 25, 30, 31, 32, 33, 34, 35, 36, 41, 67, 112, 113, 122, 123, 132, 139, 141, 142, 143, 144, 153, 155, 156
Illegal Migrants (Determination by Tribunal) Act, 1983 (IMDT), 20, 25, 30, 31, 32, 33, 34, 35, 36, 41, 67, 112, 113, 122, 123, 132, 139, 141, 142, 143, 144, 153, 155, 156
independence, 127
Indian Parliament, 4
indigenous tribes of Assam, 139
inquilab, 178
internal security threats, 144
Islamophobia, 89

Jains, 74, 113, 122, 125
Jamia Millia Islamia, 85
Janata Dal (Secular), 97
Jinnah, Mohammad Ali, 28

Kesavananda Bharati vs State of Kerala, 61
Khan, Arif Mohammad, 114
Khan, Liaquat Ali, 88, 94
Khoirabari massacre of 1983, 132

Lautenberg Amendment, 1989, 65
Lautenberg–Specter Amendment, 2004, 65
Left-wing, 114
Liberation War of 1971, 131
Local Registrar of Citizen Registration, 15

Matua community, 101, 102
Ministry of External Affairs, Government of India, 45
minority, 30, 32, 67, 87, 92, 93, 96, 98, 100, 102, 117, 119, 122, 125, 127, 139, 160, 161, 183
Modi, Narendra, 17
Mookherjee, S.P., 27, 28
Munshi, K.M., 58
Muslim League, 28, 159
Muslim migrants, 26, 30, 55, 95, 102
Myanmar, 113, 127

narrative-builders, 76, 78, 80, 83, 84, 87, 104
National Database and Registration Authority (NADRA), 4
nationalism, 76, 87, 97, 167
National Population Register (NPR), 10
National Register of Citizens (NRC), 4
National Register of Indian Citizens (NRIC), 11
Navtej Singh Johar vs Union of India, 64
Nehru, Jawaharlal, 26, 53, 72, 85, 88, 92, 166, 169
Nehru-Liaquat Pact of 1950, 88
Nellie massacre, 132
Nepali migrant, 36

Pakistan, 4, 7, 19, 21, 26–28, 31, 35, 52, 53, 55–57, 65, 67–70, 72, 74, 83, 86, 88, 89, 90, 91, 92, 93, 94, 95, 96, 97, 98, 102, 103, 110–117, 119, 121–125, 131, 140, 157, 158–165, 175
Pakistani migrant, 36
Parliamentary legislation, 170
Parsees, 67
Partition, 26, 28, 55, 57, 89–95, 97, 99, 110–112, 115–117, 123, 127, 157, 159, 160, 162, 163, 165, 166, 175
Pashtuns, 124
Passport (Entry into India) Act, 1920, 7
passport number, 18
Passport System, 113, 162
Permanent Account Number (PAN), 18
Permit System, 111, 112, 160, 162
Population Register, 10, 13, 15, 16
protest, 84, 86, 114, 169, 174, 176, 178, 180, 182, 183, 184, 186
Protocol Relating to Status of Refugees, 1967, 46
Public Distribution System (PDS), 19

Qadiani, 117

Rashtriya Swayamsevak Sangh (RSS), 74
record proof of citizenship, 146
record proof of residence, 146
Refugee Convention, 1951, 128
Registrar General of Citizens, 12, 14
Registration of Foreigners Act, 1939, 133
Registration of Foreigners Rules, 1939, 133
religious persecution, 7, 28, 35,

66, 74, 88, 97, 99, 103, 119, 125, 127, 128
Riots, 78
Rohingyas, 127

Salve, Harish, 114, 119
Santosh Kumar vs The Secretary, MHRD, 59
Sarbananda Sonowal vs Union of India, 31, 35, 142, 144
Satyagraha, 171, 181
Scheduled Castes, 72
Section 144 of the CrPC, 179
secularism, 32, 34, 50, 51, 55, 58, 59, 60, 61, 67, 69, 70, 72, 74, 114
Shah, Amit, 14, 22, 25, 84, 114, 173, 180, 181
Shaheen Bagh, 84, 85, 86, 170, 172, 173, 174, 178, 179, 180, 181, 182, 184, 185
Shayara Bano vs Union of India, 64, 88
Shias, 68, 117
Sikhs, 27, 53, 54, 74, 90, 113, 114, 115, 116, 122, 125, 127, 160, 162, 175
Singh, Manmohan, 88, 99, 100, 101
Sixth Schedule, 9, 144, 145
social media, 84
Socio-Economic Caste Census (SECC), 18

S.R. Bommai vs Union of India, 59
Sri Lanka, 113, 118, 126, 127, 175
Statement of Objects and Reasons (SOR), 122
State of Karnataka vs Dr Praveen Togadia, 59
Supreme Court of India, 25, 29, 40, 59, 61, 85, 113, 142

the case of Mahant Moti Das vs S.P. Sahi, 65
The Foreigners (Tribunals) Order, 1964 (Foreigners Tribunals), 40, 134, 135
The Independence Act of 1947, 157
Trinamool Congress (TMC), 33, 97
triple D, 132, 133, 141

UK Parliament, 157
ultra vires, 50, 63, 69, 88, 97, 143
UNHRC, 121
United Progressive Alliance (UPA), 7
Universal Declaration of Human Rights, 130

Vajpayee, Atal Bihari, 103
valid travel documents, 123
verification documents, 145
Voter ID card number, 18

Made in the USA
Monee, IL
03 May 2026